Judaistic Christianity

Judaistic Christianity

Fenton John Anthony Hort

Edited by J. O. F. Murray

BAKER BOOK HOUSE
Grand Rapids, Michigan

Reprinted 1980 by
Baker Book House Company
ISBN: 0-8010-4240-2

First published in 1894

PHOTOLITHOPRINTED BY CUSHING - MALLOY, INC.
ANN ARBOR, MICHIGAN, UNITED STATES OF AMERICA

PREFACE

DURING the last few years of Dr Hort's life he regularly chose as one of the subjects for his professorial lectures some special aspect of the history of the Apostolic and post-Apostolic age. In this way he traced at one time the various stages in the emancipation of the Church from the trammels of Judaism, and at another the gradual evolution of the conception of an Universal Ecclesia and of ecclesiastical organization. These lectures were not, I believe, primarily designed for publication, but they afforded a convenient opportunity for summarizing and bringing to a focus the results of a lifetime devoted to the patient and single-minded consideration of these fundamental questions. This volume contains the two courses which were devoted to the first of these subjects.

When the end of the academic term brought the first course to a conclusion far short of the goal which he had originally contemplated, he had just reached the discussion of the evidence to be derived from the Epistle to the Romans. As he had recently delivered a full course of lectures on the introduction to that Epistle, he had no occasion to do more than indicate the main conclusions at which he had arrived with regard to it.

The second course, after a careful recapitulation of the points already discussed, carried the treatment of the subject as far as the rise of Helxaism. Here again he reached a topic which he had already discussed in detail in a course of lectures on the Clementine *Recognitions*, and a brief reference to results already established sufficed, not indeed to fill in the whole of the outline sketched in the opening lecture of the first course, but at least to indicate his conclusions on every point of primary importance in relation to his main subject.

These lectures cover ground which has been for the last fifty years the chosen battlefield of controversialists. Yet they are not, at least in any partisan sense, controversial. They are constructive. Their object is simply to review the facts of the Apostolic history in relation to a single clearly defined issue, and to restate them in the fresh light shed on them by fifty years of free and fearless discussion.

Dr Hort had a genuine admiration for the genius of F. C. Baur, from whom the whole discussion started, and a generous appreciation of the debt that modern theology owes him for leading the way in the effort to interpret Christian documents in the light of the historical situation out of which they sprang. But he was very far from accepting Baur's conclusions. His own judgement was formed in each case independently after patient consideration of the whole evidence, and with intimate knowledge of the whole course that discussion had taken both in England and on the Continent.

His ultimate verdict, as these lectures shew, was entirely in favour of the genuineness and the historical accuracy of all the leading Christian documents. Accordingly, though he recognized frankly the force of the objections urged against the generally received tradition with regard to some of the New Testament writings, and indicated with scrupulous accuracy the different degrees of confidence with which he held particular propositions, his reconstruction follows in the main the lines with which Englishmen are traditionally familiar. What is unique in this reconstruction is the clearness with which he grasps the problem set before the Gentile Church by its relation to the Law, and his sympathetic insight into the parts played by the Apostolic leaders during the period of transition before the Old Order had finally given place to the New.

It is enough in this connexion to call attention to his analysis of the grounds of St Peter's conduct in the famous altercation at Antioch (p. 77), to his account of the incidents connected with St Paul's last visit to Jerusalem (p. 105), and above all to his subtle and masterly investigation of the character and sources of the false teaching attacked in the Epistle to the Colossians and in the Pastoral Epistles, questions on which, at least in England, Bishop Lightfoot's conclusions have perhaps too readily been accepted as final.

The views indicated in these Lectures (p. 115) with regard to the enemies of the Cross of Christ at Philippi, and to the date of the Pseudo-Clementine literature (p. 202) must await their justification in the publication of the lectures on the Introduction to the Romans, and on the Clementine *Recognitions*.

My work as editor has been simple. The lectures were written out in full before they were delivered, and they are printed here substantially as they stand in the manuscript. It proved unnecessary to print the recapitulation with which the second course began, but a few amplifications have been introduced from it into the text of the original lectures. I am responsible for all the divisions and subdivisions introduced into the text, for the titles of the separate 'lectures', and for the marginal analysis. I have verified the references, and have for the convenience of the reader printed at full length in the Appendix any that were not likely to be readily accessible.

My best thanks are due to the Rev. J. B. Mayor for kind advice and criticism during the passage of the work through the Press, and to Mr F. G. Masters, Scholar of Corpus Christi College, for help in the revision of the proof-sheets and for the compilation of the Index.

J. O. F. MURRAY

EMMANUEL COLLEGE, CAMBRIDGE
St Luke's Day, 1894

CONTENTS

VII

The Pastoral Epistles

VIII

James, 1 Peter, Hebrews, Apocalypse

IX

The Church of Jerusalem from Titus to Hadrian

X

The Judaizers of the Ignatian Epistles

XI

Cerinthus, 'Barnabas,' Justin Martyr

XII

Palestinian Ebionites

INTRODUCTORY LECTURE

THE subject on which I propose to lecture this Term is the History of Judaistic Christianity in the Apostolic and following Ages. The phrase 'Judaistic Christianity' is more ambiguous than might be wished; but it is difficult to find another more precise. To prevent any misunderstanding as to the sense in which I propose to use it, it will be well to begin with explaining what are the senses which might not unnaturally be attributed to this phrase, but which lie outside the purpose of these lectures.

The Subject of the course

First, by Judaistic Christianity I do not mean such Christianity as is Judaistic in tone and spirit only. The whole course of Church History is full of beliefs, practices, institutions, and the like, which rest on misconceptions of the true nature of the Gospel dispensation, and are in effect a falling back

Christianity not Judaistic in spirit only

after the coming of Christ to a state of things which His coming was intended to supersede, a return, as St Paul would have said, to the weak and beggarly elements. Such a Christianity however, though strictly analogous to the Judaistic Christianity of the apostolic age, is not itself strictly, i.e. historically, Judaistic. It has its origin in permanent tendencies of human nature, not chiefly or directly in imitation of Judaism, though it may borrow this or that detail from Jewish precedent.

nor by misuse of O. T.

Again, by Judaistic Christianity I do not mean such assimilations to Judaism on the part of Christians as arise from a recognition of the authority of the Old Testament unaccompanied by a clear perception of the true relation of the Old Testament to the New. A couple of comprehensive examples from different ages may be given of such assimilations resting on a crude and mechanical use of Scripture. Of this character is the eclectic appropriation of Levitical laws for the regulation of the customs of Christians, and eventually for the positive legislation of churches. This process began in the third century, and went forward with great activity after the Empire had become Christian; and we are still surrounded by its results. This was one of the elements of the mediaeval system least touched by the Reformation, the obvious reason being that the leading Reformers had themselves but an imperfect sense of the progress within Scripture, and of the different kinds of instruction which are provided for us in its several parts in accordance with God's own dispensation of times and seasons as expounded by the apostles. Thus we come to the second example of which I spoke, the appeal by the Puritans to the Jewish law and to Jewish precedents on such points as sabbath observance and the treatment of idolatry and idolaters. This was in fact a natural application of the general appeal of the Reformers from custom and tradition to Scripture, when that treatment of all Scripture as in the same sense and the same manner authoritative, was carried out consistently. This whole subject deserves much fuller investigation than it has ever received, more especially as regards the early ages of the Church; and its interest is by no means of a merely antiquarian nature. But, important as it is, it does not lie within the limits of Judaistic Christianity in the proper sense of the term. The authority so claimed was not claimed for Jewish privilege in any sense of the word, but simply for what was assumed to be absolutely Divine, and therefore of perpetual validity. Moreover, as far as our information goes, there was no historical continuity between that Christianity which as a whole was Judaistic in origin and in principle, and that crude adoption of laws recorded in the Old Testament on the part of Christians which began in the third century.

nor by dependence on O.T.

Thirdly, we may put aside that sense of the term "Judaistic Christianity" according to which nearly all Christianity may be loosely and inaccurately called Judaistic; as indeed it may with more propriety be called *Judaic*, though that too is not a happy designation. In this sense the term can be legitimately used by none but by those to whom the ideal Christianity is what is called Christianity without Judaism. In ancient times this conception of Christianity was carried out deliberately and consistently by Marcion and his school, and by no others. Unconsciously and inconsistently it has had a tolerably widespread influence, both in ancient and in modern times. The power by which, humanly speaking, it has been chiefly restrained from the earliest days to the present has been the inheritance of the ancient Scriptures. Endlessly misinterpreted and misused as the Old Testament has been in all ages, its mere presence at the head of the sacred book of the Church has remained throughout a priceless safeguard against the tendency to falsify Christianity by detaching it from the history of the Divine office of the earlier Israel. From that erroneous point of view Judaism and Christianity are two distinct religions; and in so far as Christianity retains elements derived from its predecessor it might consistently be called Judaistic. According to the apostles on the other hand the faith of Christians is but the ripening and perfection of the faith of the Old Covenant, and the Church or assembly of Christians is but the expansion of the original Israel of God, constituted by faith in Him who was Israel's Messiah.

but by ascribing universal validity to national ordinances

Briefly then we are not now concerned either with such Christianity as is Judaistic in spirit only, or secondly with such Christianity as arises from a misuse of the Old Testament due to a neglect of the order of God's Providence, or thirdly with the main stream of Christianity as resting on the basis of God's dealings with His ancient people. The only Christianity which can properly be called Judaistic is that which falls back to the Jewish point of view, belonging naturally to the time before Christ came, and still practically maintained by those Jews of subsequent ages who are not merely unbelieving members of a caste. It ascribes perpetuity to the Jewish Law, with more or less modification; thus confounding the conditions Providentially imposed for a time on the people of God when it was only a single nation, the people inhabiting Palestine,—confounding these Providential conditions with God's government of His people after its national limits were broken down and it had become universal. Judaistic Christianity, in this the true sense of the term, might with at least equal propriety be called Christian Judaism. Its position is not fundamentally or generically different from that of Mahometanism, though Jesus, not Mahomet, is its last great prophet.

Subject limited in extent

Judaistic Christianity, thus defined, is a difficult subject on account of the scantiness of the evidence still extant, but at the same time it is not of overwhelming extent. For the most part its existence is confined to the first ages of the Church; nor do I propose to say anything of such limited and obscure forms of it as have appeared in later ages. My wish is simply to give some account of one great and interesting element in early Church history, a natural product of the circumstances of the Apostolic Age, living on for some generations, and that probably not without times of revival, but becoming more and more evidently a futile anachronism as the main body of the Church grew up into a stately tree in the eyes of all men: and at length dying naturally away.

but of special interest owing to the Tübingen hypothesis

The subject would indeed be not only more extensive but very much more important, if Judaistic Christianity had really in the first and second centuries included all the Christianity which twenty or thirty years ago was so described by a great critical school on the Continent. If what is known as the Tübingen theory were true, the Christianity of the Twelve remained always Judaistic, and so also all that Christianity of the Apostolic Age which was governed by their influence. It was further a part of this theory that the Roman

Church of the second century was Judaistic in doctrine and custom, and that to this source is to be traced that organisation of the several churches, and ultimately of the Church at large, which grew up in the latter part of the second and in the third centuries. To discuss this theory in detail and with reference to all the grounds on which it has been made to rest would evidently carry us much too far away from our proper subject. But it will be worth our while to give some little attention to the supposed indications of a powerful Judaistic leaven in Christian writings other than those which came really from a Judaistic source. The reason for so doing is not strictly speaking a controversial one. The theory itself, though it has by no means lost all its indirect influence, finds much less acceptance on the Continent than it did a few years ago, and the few eminent men who still profess to uphold it have now come to clog it with so many reservations that its direct force is virtually lost. But it is difficult to understand rightly much of the biblical and historical criticism with which every one must come in contact who makes a serious study of Apostolic and early Christianity, unless we have some knowledge of the more important suppositions which have within present memory affected the interpretation of books and events, and of the grounds on which such suppositions have rested. Moreover the evidence alleged for this supposed extension of a Judaistic type of Christianity is interesting in itself, and an examination of it affords useful illustration of some important elements of ancient Christianity.

The necessity for commencing with the Gospels

The central part of our subject is that which with good reason is best known—the conflict of Judaistic Christianity with St Paul. The evidence for it lies in St Paul's own Epistles, and partly also in the Acts. To understand the nature of this conflict and the circumstances which led up to it, we must go back to that rudimentary state of the Church, so to speak, in the years immediately following the Ascension, when the brotherhood around the Apostles was confined to Jerusalem. This however is not enough. If we were to stop here, we should gain not merely a very imperfect but a very ill-proportioned view of the antecedents out of which the Christianity of the middle period of the Apostolic Age arose, and the antagonisms which it included. In other words, we must go back to the Gospels themselves, and endeavour to gather from them what evidence we can respecting our Lord's own attitude towards the institutions of the Jewish people.

Divisions of the subject

To keep exact chronological order throughout will hardly be possible consistently with clearness in the treatment of the subject. But at the outset there is every reason why we should not depart from it. The first stage then in the history will be constituted by what may be briefly called "Christ and the Law." Then will follow the relations of the Church to Judaism before the appearance of Stephen, St Stephen himself and the movement associated with his name, and the relations of the Church to Judaism between his death and the mission of Barnabas to Antioch described in Acts xi. 22—26. The Conference at Jerusalem which followed what is called St Paul's First Missionary Journey, and which is reported in Acts xv. 1—29, will occupy us next; and then the Judaizers in antagonism to St Paul stimulated by the results of his missionary labours; together with the other traces which the New Testament affords of Judaistic Christianity of a similar type. This will probably be the most convenient place for considering those books of the New Testament which have been wrongly regarded as having a Judaistic character. To complete our subject in so far as it comes within the limits of the New Testament it will then be well to examine those speculative forms of Judaistic Christianity which are condemned within its pages, that is, for the most part the doctrines of this class against which parts of the Epistle to the Colossians and of the Pastoral Epistles are directed. Returning to the main stream, if we may so call it, we shall naturally be led to the Fall of Jerusalem, and to the chief effects which it produced on Jewish Christians, not passing over altogether its effect on other Christians; and with this subject we may take what is known of immediately subsequent events in Palestine, so far as they have a bearing on Christianity. Launched on the second century, we have to deal with what some of the Fathers called Ebionism, taking account (to begin with) of the extant ancient authorities respecting it. Next will come what is known of the simpler forms of Judaistic Christianity of that period, and of its literature; and then by way of appendix the principal Christian books which have been wrongly called Judaistic, and other historical phenomena which have received attention in the same connexion. After the simpler forms of Judaistic Christianity will come, as in the case of the Apostolic Age, the speculative systems of doctrine which were in some sense Jewish or at least Samaritan, and in some sense Christian, chiefly as connected with the names of Cerinthus and Simon Magus or the Simonians. Then, and not till then, it will be time to give some brief account of the remarkable Judaistic revival called Helxaism, and of the still partially preserved Clementine literature to which it gave birth, and the Essenism from which in part it sprang. After that there will be little to detain us till we reach such evidence respecting the Jewish Christianity of the latter part of the Fourth Century and of the early part of the

Fifth as can be gathered from the ecclesiastical writers of that time. It is from them too that most of our extant evidence comes on the subject of the Gospels used by Jewish Christians of various types; and perhaps we shall find no better opportunity for trying to gather up the principal results to be obtained on this subject than this late stage of the history.

Books for students

In the matter of books recommendation is not easy. They are innumerable, and also sadly few. The book which on the whole has done most in the way of pointing towards a true understanding of the First and Second Centuries, in spite of many drawbacks, is the second edition of Ritschl's *Entstehung der altkatholischen Kirche* published in 1857. It has not been translated. We are fortunate in having his work carried on in England with thorough independence and great improvements by Bp. Lightfoot in wellknown essays in his edition of the Epistles of St Paul. The only comprehensive book accessible in English which it seems worth while to mention is the translation of Lechler's *Apostolic and Post-Apostolic Times* (2 vols., 16*s.*, Clark). In German an important and very suggestive, but as regards the N.T. unsatisfactory, book by one of the ablest of Ritschl's younger disciples is Vol. I. of Harnack's *Dogmengeschichte.* The same may be said of Weizsäcker's *Apostolisches Zeitalter* published within the last year (1887). It is also always instructive to read Ewald's *History of the*

Jewish People, i.e. for our purpose Vols. VI. and VII. translated by J. Frederick Smith. An invaluable book of reference for all kinds of illustrative facts on the Jewish side of the history is Schürer's *History of the Jewish People in the time of our Lord*. [Of this T. and T. Clark have now published a complete translation. A translation of Weizsäcker has also just appeared, and the translation of Harnack's *Grundriss* published by Hodder and Stoughton under the title of *The History of Dogma* may give English readers an outline of the contents of the more elaborate work to which allusion is made in the text.]

LECTURE II

Christ and the Law

We begin with the foundation of the early relations of Christians and their faith and practices to Judaism as laid in the relations of their Lord and Head to the Law. For our purpose it will not be necessary to examine all the passages of the Gospels which have a direct or indirect bearing on this subject; or again to consider every detail and every attendant difficulty in those passages which will come before us. It will be enough to consider the most salient points in so far as they throw light on the subsequent history.

At the outset we may pass over with a bare mention those events bringing our Lord in contact with the Jewish Law, in which others than Himself were the agents. They are the Circumcision, the Lk ii
Presentation in the Temple, the keeping the Passover at Jerusalem when He was twelve years old:—all three related by St Luke, and by him alone.

The authority of the Law

The Sermon on the Mount

It will be best to begin with that portion of our Lord's teaching which deals the most explicitly with this subject[1], the second section of the Sermon on the Mount as given by St Matthew.

The principle of Christ's relation to the Law
Mt v 17–20

"Think not that I came to destroy the law or the prophets: I came not to destroy, but to fulfil. For verily I say unto you, Till heaven and earth pass away, one jot or one tittle shall in no wise pass away from the law, till all things be accomplished. Whosoever therefore shall break one of these least commandments, and shall teach men so, shall be called least in the kingdom of heaven: but whosoever shall do and teach them, he shall be called great in the kingdom of heaven. For I say unto you, that except your righteousness shall exceed the righteousness of the scribes and Pharisees, ye shall in no wise enter into the kingdom of heaven."

is not antagonism
Mt v 17

The opening words suggest the motive from which these verses take their start. "Think not" (repeated somewhat similarly in Matt. x. 34) was not likely to have been said unless there was some real probability that without the warning the disciples might think as they are here bidden not to think. It was easy to misunderstand the true purpose of the new prophet who had appeared going about Galilee, teaching in the synagogues, proclaiming the Gospel

[1] Cf. Ewald, *Die drei ersten Evangelien*, pp 263 f. See Appendix.

of the kingdom, and healing all manner of sickness and infirmity. Signs of His coming antagonism to Scribes and Pharisees, the jealous guardians of the Law, had possibly already appeared. At all events the tone and drift of His teaching was manifestly unlike theirs. Thus it was not unnatural to assume hastily that it was a purpose of His mission simply to break down restraints, to lift from men's shoulders the duties which they felt as burdens. The Law was full of commandments which claimed to be obeyed. The Prophets were full of rebukes of transgressors, and warnings of coming doom. Might not the mild new Rabbi be welcomed as one come to break down the Law and the Prophets, and so lead the way to easier and less exacting ways of life?

but fulfilment

This is the delusion which our Lord set Himself to crush. The Gospel of the kingdom was not a Gospel of indulgence. "Think not that I came to destroy the Law or the Prophets (to pull them down, undo them:—both these shades of meaning meet in *καταλῦσαι*): I came not to destroy but to fulfil." These last two verbs are doubtless absolute: not as regards Law and Prophets only, but as regards all things, not destruction but fulfilment was His characteristic work. But this was especially true for the Law and the Prophets. About the word "fulfil" (*πληρῶσαι*) there is a certain ambiguity. But we may safely neglect the meaning which perhaps comes first to mind, that of personal obedience or performance,

as we speak of the fulfilment of an injunction. The true meaning answers much more exactly to that destroying or undoing to which it is here formally opposed. It is to bring to fulness or completion, involving therefore a progress: it is not to keep a thing as it was. In the same sense, with reference to
Rom xiii 8, 10 the same subject, St Paul says *ὁ γὰρ ἀγαπῶν τὸν ἕτερον νόμον πεπλήρωκεν*, and *πλήρωμα οὖν νόμου*
Gal v 14 *ἡ ἀγάπη*; and again *ὁ γὰρ πᾶς νόμος ἐν ἑνὶ λόγῳ πεπλήρωται, ἐν τῷ Ἀγαπήσεις τὸν πλησίον σου ὡς σεαυτόν*. What kind of bringing to fulness or completion was meant would appear shortly after.

of an eternal purpose The next verse goes back behind Christ's own present purpose to the eternal purpose of His Father. It would have been monstrous that He should have set Himself to destroy or undo that which was destined to live as long as heaven and earth. "For
Mt v 18 verily I say unto you, Till heaven and earth pass away, one jot or one tittle shall in no wise pass away till all be come to pass." The precise force of these last words (*ἕως ἂν πάντα γένηται*) is not quite clear: they probably mean "till all has come to pass that is involved in the purpose of the Law", cf. the
Lk xvi 17 form given to the saying in St Luke "It is easier for heaven and earth to pass away, than for one tittle of the law to fall."

The Teacher's responsibility Next our Lord warns His disciples "Whosoever
Mt v 19 therefore shall *loose* one of these least commandments, and shall teach men so, shall be called least in

the kingdom of heaven: but whosoever shall do and teach them, he shall be called great in the kingdom of heaven." Λύσῃ probably does not mean 'break' here, if indeed it ever does, but rather 'loose', i.e. relax, weaken and dissolve the hold which a commandment has on men's consciences and wills. Of course personal violation of a commandment would be one way of loosing. While καταλῦσαι stands for what might have been the powerful and decisive purpose of a prophet or reformer, λύσῃ stands for the lesser acts of disciples tending in the same direction. In many ways the commandments might be weakened by more or less indirect disparagement through word or deed, and then there might come also the deliberate teaching ("and teach men so"). He who does this was to be called least in the kingdom of heaven. This cannot mean exclusion from the kingdom of heaven; and so the only reasonable inference is that such disparagement of a commandment might be compatible with general loyalty to the Law; that is, that it might find some *seeming* justification in the true meaning of Christ's teaching; though only the disciple who did perfect homage in both act and word was to be called great in the kingdom of heaven. Then came the tremendous warning which winds up these introductory verses, "For I say unto you that except your Mt v 20
righteousness shall exceed the righteousness of the Scribes and Pharisees, ye shall in no wise enter into the kingdom of heaven". That is, the Gospel calls

not for less righteousness, but for more righteousness than was practised by the professed devotees of the Law. Not, that is, that it heaps on more precepts, making itself a Law of multiplied and minuter enactments, but that it demands another order of righteousness, as it were penetrating deeper and rising higher.

'Fulfilment' illustrated Mt v 21 ff. Then come instances by which the more abounding righteousness of the Gospel is illustrated. "Ye have heard that it was said to them of old time" is the usual formula which introduces some precept of the Law, with or without modification or addition supplied by tradition. In each case a new teaching "But I say unto you" is set up over against the ancient teaching. These examples and the introductory verses explain each other, as they were evidently meant to do. What was said to them of old time was not to be destroyed but fulfilled. It remained binding within its own limits, but it was to be filled out and deepened by a new spirit, the prohibition of murder for instance being fulfilled by the prohibition of anger against a brother. What is here implied is that behind the Law in its original form there lay a Divine purpose for the Law, and that the fulfilment of the Law, in this pregnant sense of the word fulfilment, was an accomplishment of that Divine purpose.

after the likeness of the Father Mt v 43-48 The last of the six examples in particular carries us up to God Himself. The very commandment to love one's neighbour is here set forth as needing to be fulfilled by a more comprehensive love, including even enemies, after the likeness of the Father in heaven, Who maketh His sun to rise on the evil and the good. The concluding verse of this example, rising naturally out of that reference to the Father's impartial grace, makes also a deeply instructive conclusion to the whole of this section on the Law. "Ye therefore shall be perfect, as your heavenly Father is perfect." Not only is the true foundation indicated for the truer and more perfect type of love which is our Lord's immediate subject here; but the principle is set forth which gives the Gospel righteousness its pre-eminence as compared with the righteousness prescribed of old time. From what God commands it rises to what God *is*: His own perfection, so far as human faculties can behold it, is the standard and the power of human perfection. This *is* the fulfilment of the Law.

The application of the principle

Here then we have the *principle* of Christ's relation to the Law. Some of the difficulties connected with its application and some instances of its application will next come before us.

The Golden Rule

Before we leave the Sermon on the Mount it is well to notice one verse in its later part, which is in effect an application of the principle already laid down. The section which begins "Judge not that ye be not judged", after travelling over various ground, the connexion of the parts of which we need not now discuss, ends with the broad commandment

Mt vii 1–12

"All things therefore whatsoever ye would that men should do unto you, even so do ye also unto them, for this is the Law and the Prophets." The verse contains two parts, the precept and the reason given for it. The precept without the reason occurs again with slightly modified language in Luke vi. 31, there too as part of the Sermon on the Mount but in a somewhat different connexion, the preceding verse answering to Matthew v. 42. A negative precept answering to this, but differing essentially in being only negative, a prohibition of evil doing, not a positive principle of well doing, seems to have been already current among the Jews at least from the time when Tobit was written, and indeed among the Greeks; and in this form was added by the Western
Ac xv 20, 29 text to the letter from the Jewish Conference to the Gentile converts. Nay, it is attributed to the R. Hillel[1], who lived just before the Christian era, in a form which includes an idea corresponding to the reason given in the second clause. "A foreigner came to Shammai to be converted provided that he could be taught the whole Thorah whilst he stood on one foot." Shammai beat him away, and he went to Hillel, who said "What is hateful to thyself do not to thy fellow: this is the whole Thorah, and the rest is commentary: go, study." Our Lord's words, addressed not to an impatient would-be proselyte, but to His own Jewish disciples, were

[1] Cf. C. Taylor in *Pirqe Aboth* i. 16 n. 33.

doubtless intended not merely to teach the precept but to teach it as a fulfilment of the Law and the Prophets, not as at once superseding them. In this connexion notice the double phrase "Law *and* Prophets." The two are taken together as together making up the inherited Divine instrument of teaching and guidance, whereas before they were divided by '*or*', and thus each separately received from Christ its own sanction. He was no champion of the Law against the Prophets, or of the Prophets against the Law. The ground on which He declared Himself their fulfiller was common to both alike.

The Great Commandment

Once more, at a later period of the Ministry, when our Lord, in answer to the lawyer's question as to a first or great commandment in the Law (to which we shall have to return presently for another purpose), named the love of God and the love of neighbour, He added, "On these two commandments the whole Law hangeth and the Prophets." (Mt xxii 40) The question had been on the Law, and to that the answer was primarily addressed, but the Prophets were significantly added afterwards. Here the word ὅλος carries us a step beyond the former conclusion, and that in two ways. Doing to others as we would have them do to us is after all no more than a rule of conduct, the Golden Rule, as it is sometimes called. But *love* of neighbour goes deeper, to a principle below the rule, to a permanent attitude of mind. And again this comprehensive statement is made not of love of neighbour alone but of that and love of God conjointly. Here then we find laid down in all its completeness that fulfilling of the Law and the Prophets of which Christ spoke at the outset.

John the Baptist

Next we may take some of our Lord's language respecting John the Baptist. His relation to John is a very peculiar one. In the New Testament John occupies a much more prominent place than he does in our ordinary thoughts about the Gospel history. We must not linger over the Baptism, or the witness of John recorded in the opening chapter of the Fourth Gospel, or his other testimony given on the occasion of the dispute of his disciples with a Jew about purification. But we must not forget the double aspect which our Lord's relation to John presents throughout these records: the close connexion on the one hand, not of kinship only but of office, in which our Lord is in some sense a receiver at the hands of John, and on the other hand the deep line of demarcation, not of nature or of office only, but, as growing out of these, of the periods or dispensations to which they respectively belong; the one the end of the past, the Other the Beginning of the future.

Relationship twofold, connexion and contrast

Jn i 30 f.

Jn iii 22–30

Discussion with John's disciples

The first utterance of Christ which we need examine arose out of a question asked or comment made on the fact that His disciples were not fasting at some particular time (probably one of the fasts occurring twice a week according to Jewish tradition), although the Baptist's disciples agreed with the Pharisees in keeping this fast. The immediate answer justifies Christ's disciples without condemning John's disciples. The practice of Christ's own disciples is deduced from their own special position as sons of the bridechamber, not from any universal duty. Around the bridegroom, the living embodiment of the new communion between God and man (on which designation cf. John's own words in John iii. 29), were gathered his chosen friends, the sons of the bridechamber, as they were called. Apparently by Rabbinic custom[1] all in attendance on the bridegroom were dispensed from certain religious observances in consideration of their duty to increase his joy. And so the special new joy of the kingdom of heaven in which they were ministers made the present time a time unfit for fasting, in so far as it was an expression of sorrow, though days of bereavement were coming in which it would be appropriate enough. Here then we have the kingdom of heaven exhibited as of higher authority than sacred custom; but this is not laid down as holding good except for those who had personally received the kingdom.

Mt ix 14, 15 Mk ii 18-20 Lk v 33-35

Then come two well-known but very difficult parabolic sayings, that of the piece of undressed cloth on an old garment, and of the new wine in old wine-skins.

Mt ix 16, 17 Mk ii 21, 22 Lk v 36-38

[1] Cf. Meuschen p. 80 f. Novum Testamentum ex Talmude et antiquitatibus Hebraeorum illustratum. Lipsiae 1736. Appendix.

The most probable interpretation is I think that of Weiss, viz. that having justified His own disciples, our Lord goes on to explain why He does not thereby condemn John's disciples. They still belonged to the old order of things preceding the coming of the kingdom of heaven; and it would be incongruous and unprofitable if, while so remaining, they borrowed some practice fitting only for the sons of the new kingdom, or still more some new spirit such as was expressed in the new practice. Thus far all three evangelists use substantially the same language. An additional saying is however preserved by St Luke (v. 39), [if, as is *possible*, though not likely, it is not his own, being omitted by the chief Western documents, it is evidently at least a relic of a very early and trustworthy tradition,] "And no man having drunk old [wine] desireth new, for he saith The old is good". Here the probable meaning comes out still more clearly. It was no mere unbelief that kept John's disciples from drinking the new wine of the Gospel. They did not deliberately set the one against the other (χρηστός, not χρηστότερος, is certainly the true reading); but in the revival and repentance due to John's preaching they had found the old order good, as indeed it was, and so they craved nothing more.

The result of the discussion

Thus the whole incident and comment on it bring before us another aspect of our Lord's position. The new here is not the fulfilment of the old, but its advancing successor, while yet adhesion to the old is set forth as not in itself blameable, nor the old itself as otherwise than good. Again, we cannot safely say that the old is here identical with the Law; for the fasting which gave rise to the incident was not commanded by the Law but by a later tradition. On the other hand we read here no condemnation of this tradition, as we do elsewhere of some other analogous traditions. Its precise relation to the Law in our Lord's estimation remains undefined.

Christ's testimony to the Baptist
Mt xi 2–19
Lk vii 18–35

Next comes the passage which contains the fullest and most express statement respecting the Baptist. John hears in the prison concerning those acts of our Lord which were in the truest sense, whether John at this time recognised them as such or not, *τὰ ἔργα τοῦ χριστοῦ*, the characteristic works of the Messiah. He sends disciples to ask Jesus about Himself, and the answer is given by a recital of these works, ending with the significant warning in the form of a beatitude, "And happy is he who shall find none occasion of stumbling in me." Then, as the messengers depart, Christ questions and instructs the multitudes about the Baptist. For our purpose we need notice only the latter words: "A prophet, yea I say unto you and much more than a prophet: this is he of whom it is written 'Behold I send my messenger before thy face, who shall prepare thy way before thee'." A moment's reflection on what is involved in these words will show to what a singularly high position they lift the Baptist, and how in the same breath they exhibit his office as a wholly subsidiary and preparatory one, making but a way for the coming of the Being whom (in this form of the quotation) Jehovah addresses as pre-eminently "coming". Then the same sharp antithesis is repeated in a totally different form. None greater than the Baptist hath been raised up among them born of women, yet great though he be, he is less than the least in the kingdom of heaven.

A new period now begun

Here the two records diverge for a few lines. St Matthew (xi. 12 f.) continues our Lord's words with two closely connected sayings which reappear in inverted order in a different context of St Luke (xvi. 16). "But from the days of John the Baptist until now the kingdom of heaven suffereth violence, and men of violence take it by force" (or, in Luke's report, "from that time [the time of John] the Gospel of the kingdom of God is preached, and every man entereth violently into it"). Whatever else these difficult words contain, at least they express that a new period, that of the kingdom of heaven, had set in after what are called the days of John the Baptist, and that his preaching had led to a violent and impetuous thronging to gather round Jesus and His disciples, a thronging in which our Lord apparently saw as much unhealthy excitement as true conviction.

John the close of the old

Then He goes on "For all the Prophets and the Law prophesied until John". The word 'prophesied', which is omitted in Luke's report, may be variously understood. What concerns us now is common to both Gospels, that John is distinctly marked as closing the age of all the Prophets and of the Law, which for this purpose is treated as itself "prophetic". The same is implied in yet another sentence added in Matthew alone (xi. 14), "And if ye are willing to receive [it], this is Elijah which is (or was) to come", as also in the fuller saying uttered soon after the Transfiguration, on Elijah coming first, i.e. as being the immediate precursor of the Coming of the Lord. And to return to the passage in Matthew xi. 16—19, Luke vii. 31—35, the rebuke to "the men of this generation" for their impartial rejection of John the abstinent recluse and of Christ who companied with men is indirectly a vindication of John in relation to his appointed place. A similar vindication of both missions is virtually contained in the question asked of the high priests, scribes, and elders, "The baptism of John, whence was it? from heaven or from men?" more especially in connexion with our Lord's comment on the parable of the two sons, which follows immediately in Matthew (xxi. 28—32).

Mt xvii 10–13 Mk ix 11–13

Mt xxi 23–27 Mk xi 27–33 Lk xx 1–8

Summary

To gather up briefly the substance of these passages of the Gospels on the Baptist: they agree with the passages on the Law and Prophets in testifying to a divinely appointed function of the Forerunner himself, and indirectly of the whole old dispensation which was represented by him: and they exhibit the new order as a better order succeeding an order which was good though far less good. On the other hand they are silent on the fulfilment of the old by the new, and therefore they are also silent on what goes along with that idea of fulfilment, the ideal perpetuity of the Old, the indestructibility of the Law and the Prophets.

The Interpretation of the Law

Scribes and Pharisees

The subject is so large that we must hasten rapidly on now. As John the Baptist stands for the worthy representative of the Law and the Prophets under the old order, so the Scribes and Pharisees stand for its unworthy representatives. The picture of them in the Gospels is a complex one, and some important elements of it are too indirectly connected with our subject to occupy us. The moral and religious faults charged against them must not be confounded with their relations to the Law or even to tradition as teachers: but we must also remember that our Lord's words point to their casuistry, their exaggerated insistance on trifles of formality, and their preference of tradition as such to the original Law, as being only other fruits of the same corrupt tree which produced their hypocrisy and hardness of heart. This explains the apparent inconsistency of His language respecting them.

the authorised interpreters

Speaking to the multitudes and to the disciples, He emphatically sanctions their authority: "The Scribes and the Pharisees sit (rather, have taken their seat, i.e. as judges) on Moses' seat: all things therefore whatsoever they bid you, [these] do and observe"; while He proceeds "but do not ye after their works, for they say and do not". There is here probably a reference to Deut. xvii. 10 f., which was we know[1] quoted against disobedience to what were called the precepts of the elders. At all events Christ here inculcates deference to their oral teaching, while elsewhere He charges them with making void the Word (or Law or Commandment) of God because of their tradition; and said in reference to them "Every plant which My Heavenly Father hath not planted shall be rooted up", calling them also "blind guides". He taught no rebellion against their precepts as positive rules, but He condemned the spirit of their teaching as contradictory to the Law and the Prophets. It is apparently from this point of view that He not only defends His disciples for eating bread with unwashed hands, but lays down broadly the impossibility of real defilement through anything which enters into a man, though such a principle would be applicable to various Levitical laws as well as to later traditions. He condemned neither the washings nor the differences of meats, but He did strenuously condemn the confusion of such mere rules with principles of religion and morality, i.e.

Mt xxiii 2

Mt xv 3, 6
Mk vii 9, 13

Mt xv 13 f.

and their precepts

[1] See *Tanchuma*, fol. 63, 2, apud Schöttgen, *Hor. Hebr.* p. 136.

with the substance of the Law and the Prophets, and He defended the violation of such rules, not as a habit but when the cause was adequate.

Instances of conformity
Mt viii 4
Mk i 44
Lk v 14

It was therefore no inconsistency when He bade the cleansed leper shew himself to the priest and make the offering prescribed by the Law. Here there was no perverse teaching intervening to confuse the issue. A man still under the Law, though he had approached in faith, was simply instructed to obey the Law, and thereby at the same time to carry his gratitude to the supreme Author of his healing.

Mt xvii 24–27

Similarly He directed St Peter to pay on behalf of both of them the half shekel levied for the temple service, "lest", He said, "we cause them to stumble"; while He instructed the apostle privately that the new relations created by the kingdom of heaven had abolished for its children the occasion of the claim for payment. That is, He deliberately conformed to the obligations of the old order, though He taught a chosen disciple that their truest allegiance was now due to a different order, an order which set them free from this particular obligation, though only to claim them for a more comprehensive service.

Relative importance of different parts of the Law

It is sometimes said that Christ abolished the ceremonial part of the Law, while He maintained the moral part of it, i.e. either the Ten Commandments, or these Ten together with the other moral prohibitions contained in it. But this view is by no

means borne out by the testimony of the Gospels. The second table (to use our phrase) of what we call the Ten Commandments (properly the Ten 'Words,' according to both Old Testament and Jewish usage) is once cited by our Lord in reply to the young ruler, who Mt xix 18 f. Mk x 19
seems to have expected to learn from Him some pecu- Lk xviii 20
liar single secret for attaining eternal life, but in a manner which indicates only a special adaptation to the circumstances of his case. Nothing of the kind occurs in the passages of wider bearing respecting the Law which we have been considering, or elsewhere. Nay, in the Sermon on the Mount the first two Mt v 21, 27
examples of what was said to them of old time, in contrast to the fulfilment brought by Christ Himself, are the Commandments against murder and against adultery. The difference which Christ does lay down within the Law is wholly different from this supposed difference of ceremonial and moral precepts. He opposes the tithing of mint, anise, and Mt xxiii 23
cummin to leaving undone the *weightier matters* of cf. Lk xi 42
the Law, judgment and mercy and faith, not, be it observed, *prohibitions* at all, whether taken from the Ten Commandments or from any other legal source, but three positive habits of mind and conduct which had been singled out by two prophets. Hosea had Hos xii 6
said "Therefore turn thou to thy God: keep mercy and judgment and wait on thy God continually", and Micah "He hath shewed thee, O man, what is good; Mic vi 8
and what doth the Lord require of thee but to do justly

and to love mercy and to walk humbly with thy God?" Still more significant perhaps is the manner in which one of these three weightier matters of the Law was singled out on two occasions, as it stands embodied in the trenchant prophetic words of Hosea vi. 6, "I desire mercy and not sacrifice".
Mt ix 13 Our Lord quoted it first in vindication of His own eating with publicans and sinners, as forbidding Him to shrink from ceremonial defilement if such shrinking would restrain Him from coming nigh to the spiritually sick as their physician. He quoted it
Mt xii 7 again in vindication of His disciples' eating the ears of corn in their hunger while passing through the cornfields on the Sabbath, as sanctioning the breach of a traditional mode of observance to relieve a real human need. In neither case was a literal sacrifice set aside for the sake of mercy: but the principle asserted by the prophet in relative disparagement of even the most sacred of all ceremonial or legal acts was reaffirmed by our Lord as applying to other customs or laws.

The Sabbath Mt xii 1–13 Mk ii 23–iii 5 Lk vi 1–11 xiii 10–17 xiv 1–6 Jn v 9 18

It would take us too long to examine the series of our Lord's words and deeds in reference to the Sabbath, itself, be it remembered, an institution embodied with special solemnity in the Decalogue. Assuredly He taught no abolition of it. The authority which He claimed when He declared the Son of Man to be Lord of the Sabbath was not, we may be sure, authority to abolish or to retain it; but authority to follow its true meaning in contravention, if necessary, of traditional rules for its observance. He seeks to associate it with the beneficent work of healing and restoration, because this was to give it new life in accordance with its proper meaning. His Sabbath acts are so many *fulfillings*, to use His own word, of the Sabbath law.

Marriage and Divorce

Once more, we have an example of the same principle, differing in form rather than in substance, in His treatment of another sacred and fundamental law, the law of marriage. He pronounced the Levitical regulation of divorce to have been given for the hardness of men's hearts; a pregnant judgment, doubtless intended to be extended to many other subjects; but He did not abolish it. What He did was to go back to the underlying principle of marriage as actually expressed at the ideal beginning of human society, and to point to that principle, apart from all human or divine legislation, as supplying the only true answer to the question of the Pharisees.

Mt v 31 f. xix 3–12 Mk x 2–12

Gen ii 24

The House of Israel

Limitations of the earthly ministry

We have now considered the most important passages of the Gospels bearing on our Lord's relation to the Law. But we must not altogether pass over the evidence as to His relation to the Jewish nation and to other nations. The starting-point is the comprehensive fact that, so far as we know, His work was almost wholly confined within the limits of the Jewish land and the Jewish population, and therefore subject to the conditions naturally arising from this limitation. To think of His position or His mission as promiscuously cosmopolitan is to cut Him off not only from the Old Testament but from all the historical circumstances of His Incarnation. This consideration gives fresh force to His injunction to the Twelve, "Go not into any way of the Gentiles, and enter not into any city of the Samaritans; but go rather to the lost sheep of the house of Israel". We might have thought the injunction not necessary, but the absence of a practical need of it throws only the more stress on it as conveying a thought with which it was well to charge the Apostles' minds. In the healing of the daughter of the Canaanite woman in the region of Tyre, we listen to the Lord's account of His own mission (Matthew xv. 24), in the words "I was not sent but unto the lost sheep of the house of Israel"; nor is there any ground for regarding these and the following words as merely intended for a trial of the woman's faith, though they served that purpose likewise. When at length the boon is granted her, nothing is said to take away from its exceptional and as it were extraneous character: it remains a crumb from the children's table. The true view is admirably expressed

Mt x 5 f.

by Ewald, "In this Jesus shewed Himself doubly great, first in the deliberate firm limitation to His immediate calling, then in the equally deliberate overstepping of these limits so soon as this was recommended by a higher consideration, and as by way of previous indication for a more distant future, in which the present limits may become extinct". *Drei erst. Evv.* p. 328

Hints of a coming extension

But along with this resolute concentration upon Jewish ground, the Gospels bear ample testimony to the intended extension of the kingdom of heaven hereafter. Our thoughts naturally turn to such passages in St John's Gospel as "Other sheep I have, which are not of this fold: them also I must bring, and they shall hear my voice", a saying suggested by the thought of the Passion, "I lay down my life for the sheep": and again to the coming of Greeks through Philip to our Lord leading to some specially solemn words, including the saying, again referring to the Passion, "I, if I be lifted up from the earth, will draw all men unto myself". But teaching to the same general effect is recorded in the other Gospels, as "Many shall come from the East and from the West, and shall sit down with Abraham, and Isaac, and Jacob, in the kingdom of heaven", being in Matthew suggested by the Centurion's faith, pronounced to be such as our Lord had not found "even in Israel". And similar language is to be found in a series of the later parables,

Jn x 16

Jn x 15

Jn xii 20 ff.

Mt viii 11 f. cf. Lk xiii 29

Mt xxi 43 as in 'the Vineyard and the Husbandmen' "The
kingdom of God shall be taken away from you, and
shall be given to a nation bringing forth the fruits
Mt xxii 9 thereof", in 'the Marriage Feast', and most emphati-
Mt xxv 32 cally of all, in 'the Sheep and the Goats', according
to its true interpretation as a judgment of the nations.
So also the great apocalyptic discourse in all three
Mt xxiv 2 Synoptic Gospels is introduced by a prediction of the
Mk xiii 2 Lk xxi 6 destruction of the temple, and further on Christ
Mt xxiv 14 declares that "this Gospel of the kingdom shall be
cf. Mk xiii 10 proclaimed in all the world for a testimony to all the
nations, and then shall come the end". The words
about the temple must be taken in connexion with
Jn ii 19 the utterance "Destroy (λύσατε) this temple, and in
three days I will raise it up", and with the accusation
Mt xxvi 61 —doubtless a perversion of real words—"This man
cf. xxvii 40 said, I am able to destroy (καταλῦσαι) the temple of
God, and to build it up in three days", or as St Mark
Mk xiv 58 gives it, "We heard him say, I will destroy (ἐγὼ κατα-
cf. xv 29 λύσω) this temple that is made with hands, and in
three days I will build another made without hands"
—the first person of the rebuilding being in the accu-
sation transferred likewise to the destruction.

Summary of the Gospel evidence Thus, to put in few words the chief deductions from the Gospel evidence, our Lord declared Himself not the destroyer of the Law and the Prophets but their fulfiller, in that He sought to give effect to their true purpose and inner meaning. He indicated that for Himself and His true disciples the old form of the Law had ceased to be binding: but He did not disobey its precepts or even the precepts of tradition, or encourage His disciples to do so, except in so far as obedience would have promoted that Pharisaic misuse of the Law and of tradition alike, which called forth His warmest denunciations. Nay, He did homage to that (for its time) right service of the old order which was represented by John the Baptist, though He at the same time proclaimed its entirely lower and transitory character. Again, Christ deliberately confined His own ministry and that of His Apostles within Jewish limits, except in a case or two distinctly exceptional; while He clearly made known that the privileges of the people of God were to be extended to mankind. This twofold character of our Lord's action and teaching, recurring under different forms, specially attested in Matthew, the most Judaic of all the Gospels, foreshadows the only way in which the Divine purpose, humanly speaking, could be accomplished; while it was inevitably open to much misunderstanding on the one side and on the other. The fundamental point, a fulfilment of the Law which was not a literal retention of it as a code of commandments was as it is still a conception hard to grasp: it was easier either to perpetuate the conditions of the old covenant or else to blaspheme them. Again there was ample matter for apparent contradictions in the necessity for a time

of transition during which the old order would live on by the side of the new, not Divinely deprived of its ancient sanctity, and yet laid under a Divine warning of not distant extinction. This period of transition was
Jn iii 30 prefigured in the Baptist's own testimony: "He must increase, but I must decrease"—decrease, not simply give way and be gone; the end of the old order and the beginning of the new were to overlap, not to be divided by an abrupt succession. Hence part of our Lord's action and teaching had reference to what was permanent in the new order of which He was the Head and Foundation; part of it had reference to temporary requirements of present circumstances, but it was easy to confound the one with the other, and not easy to distinguish them in due proportion. The great point to remember is that it was hardly possible for either aspect to be forgotten in men's recollections of the original Gospel at any period of the Apostolic age, however vaguely and confusedly both might be apprehended.

LECTURE III

THE EARLY CHURCH AT JERUSALEM

The final injunctions of the Risen Lord

Two of the Gospels in their genuine texts record final injunctions of our Lord to the Eleven, with or without other disciples, with explicit reference to the universality of their mission. In St Matthew we read "All authority is given Me in heaven and on earth: go ye *therefore* (since the authority of Messiah on earth was not partial or national only, but universal), go ye therefore and bring all the nations into discipleship (μαθητεύσατε πάντα τὰ ἔθνη)". And an echo of this form of the command is preserved in the appendix to St Mark, "Go ye (πορευθέντες, as in St Matthew) into all the world and proclaim the Gospel to the whole creation". In St Luke the charge is developed further, "And that repentance and remission of sins should be preached in His name unto all the nations, beginning from Jerusalem. Ye are witnesses of these things", and again "but tarry ye in the city until ye be clothed with power from on high". Here the ultimate sphere, all the nations, and the immediate sphere,—sphere as well as starting-place, as ἀρξάμενοι implies,—viz. Jerusalem,

Mt xxviii 18 f.

[Mk] xvi 15

Lk xxiv 47, 49

are brought out with equal distinctness. The only condition for the transition from the one sphere to the other is the having been clothed with power from on high. In the last words of the Gospel we read Lk xxiv 52 f. that as the Lord parted from the disciples, "they worshipped Him, and returned to Jerusalem with great joy, and were continually in *the temple,* blessing God". The same twofold charge recurs in the open-Ac i 4 f. ing verses of the Acts. "He charged them (the Apostles) not to depart from Jerusalem but to wait for the promise of the Father", which He explained as 'baptism with the Holy Ghost' not many days Ac i 8 hence. And again, "but ye shall receive power, when the Holy Ghost is come upon you (or, by the coming of the Holy Ghost upon you), and ye shall be my witnesses both in Jerusalem and in all Judea and Samaria, *and unto the uttermost part of the earth.*"

Ac i 12 To Jerusalem then they returned after the Ascension, and there awaited the next national feast. At Ac i 14 this time their perseverance in prayer is spoken of, but nothing is said of any preaching.

The Day of Pentecost Ac ii Then came the great event of the Day of Pentecost, the outpouring of the Spirit as manifested by wondrous typical gifts. The description of the various classes of spectators here at the outset of the history reminds us of the vast extent of the Jewish dispersion, and of the consequent multiplicity of channels through which the Gospel was hereafter to make its way among the nations. The presence of hearers of many

names from a wide extent of Asia, besides two from the Hellenized N.E. of Africa (Egypt and Cyrene), and one, but that one from the mother-city of the Empire, from Europe, could not but be a living reminder of the future apostolic work, though, as was natural, none apparently were there but Jews settled away from Judea, or proselytes, whom they had made from the Gentiles, not Gentiles in creed as well as race. It might perhaps have been expected that when once this miraculous inauguration, as it were, of the apostolic mission had taken place, some steps would immediately be taken for going forth into other lands, as some at least of our Lord's words might seem to e.g. Lk
direct. But no sign of any such movement is re- xxiv 49
corded by St Luke; and the reason of the delay was probably the duty of proclaiming the Gospel systematically and strenuously to the Jewish people, as the first and most necessary step of the impending work.

St Peter's appeal

The full range of future recipients of the Gospel is distinctly recognised by St Peter in the exhortation to repentance and baptism which he addressed to the Jews who had been pricked to the heart by his discourse on that great day, addressed, we are told, to the Jews and to all the inhabitants of Jeru- Ac ii 14
salem. "The promise is to you and to your children Ac ii 39
and to *all that are afar off*, even as many as the Lord our God shall call unto Him". But the exhortation is not "Come out of Israel", as though the people or the city had become an obsolete or an evil thing.

Ac ii 40 "Save yourselves", St Peter says, "from this crooked generation", i.e. from the present unworthy representatives of Israel; the phrase being taken[1] from the Deut xxxii 5 description of the rebellious Israelites in the desert, Mt xvii 17 Lk ix 41 partially used also by our Lord Himself. About 3000 souls, we read, were added on that day; the same by no means obvious verb, προστίθεμαι, being cf. Ac v 14, xi 24 used (here and elsewhere in Acts) which the LXX. has in Is. xiv. 1 for a proselyte who is joined to Israel.

The manner of life of the new converts Ac ii 42 The next verse, describing their manner of life, is very important, but not free from ambiguity. "And they were continuing steadfastly with the teaching of the Apostles and with the communion, with the breaking of the bread and with the prayers". Among these four terms there is none which directly suggests any Jewish observance, while the first, the teaching of the Apostles, is obviously Christian. The only natural interpretation of the four is as together constituting the characteristic marks of the new Christian life which they had taken up. Respecting the continued adherence to Jewish observances, nothing is said which implies either its *'The teaching'* presence or its absence. 'The teaching of the Apostles' was the necessary instrumentality for bringing the new converts to full discipleship. Their rudimentary faith needed a careful and continuous instruction, an instruction which replaced that which the scribes were in the habit of giving, so that in the most

[1] Cf. Lightfoot on Phil. ii. 15.

literal sense the Apostles might now be called scribes Mt xiii 52
become disciples to the kingdom, bringing out of their treasure things new and old, the new tale of the ministry and glory of Jesus, the old promises and signs by which Law and Prophets had pointed onward to Him and His kingdom.

'The communion'

The next term, 'the communion' (τῇ κοινωνίᾳ) is less clear. The order of the words excludes the connexion with τῶν ἀποστόλων adopted by the Authorised Version and the Revised Version (text), which is also unnatural here in sense. Yet something more external and concrete than a spirit of communion is required by parallelism with the other three terms. It must be some outward expression of the new fellowship[1] with the general body of Christian believers, answering to the special relation to the Apostles. The form which this fellowship took was doubtless the treatment of property as a thing not to be held without reference to the needs of the destitute among the community, and a consequent contribution to their maintenance. The help thus given was apparently not in money but in public Ac vi 1
meals, such as from another point of view are called cf. vi 2 τραπέζαις
'the daily ministration'.

'The breaking of the bread'

The 'breaking of the bread' is of course what we call the Holy Communion in its primitive form as an Agape or Supper of Communion.

[1] For analogous and equally concrete senses of κοινωνία cf. e.g. Rom. xv. 26, Heb. xiii. 16, and Lightfoot's note on Phil. i. 5.

'The prayers'

'The prayers are probably Christian prayers at stated hours, answering to Jewish prayers. If we knew more of the synagogue services in Palestine as they were before the Fall of Jerusalem, we should perhaps find that these Christian prayers replaced synagogue prayers, (which it must be remembered are not recognised in the Law,) as the Apostles' teaching may be supposed to have replaced that of the scribes.

Life in the Early Church
Ac ii 44–47

What is said in the next verses is said not of the new converts only, but of "all that believed". Their life towards each other was exhibited in the qualified and guarded community of goods which they practised. Their life towards God was exhibited in their continuing steadfastly with one accord in the temple and breaking bread in private houses (*κατ' οἶκον*), both of them acts of fellowship with men as well as with God. How far their participation in the use of the temple went, we are not told. With the single very peculiar exception of the ceremonies and oblations with which St Paul accompanied 'the four men having a vow' at his last visit to Jerusalem, there is no record of any kind of connexion between the Apostles or any other Christians and any kind of sacrificial act. Yet that incident seems to imply that similar acts were not uncommon among the Christians of Jerusalem, and indeed it is difficult to understand how they could have been omitted at Jerusalem without a deliberate breach with the Jewish people. But at

Ac xxi 26

all events we have distinct evidence that Christian Jews like other Jews frequented the temple, the sanctuary of the nation, and thereby maintained their claim to be Jews in a true sense. Accordingly as the last words of St Luke's Gospel spoke of the disciples as continually in the temple, blessing God, so we read of St Peter and St John going up to the temple at the hour of prayer, the ninth hour; and again of all (apparently, all the Christians) being with one accord in Solomon's porch. So also, when the imprisoned Apostles were released by an angel, he bid them go and stand and speak *in the temple* to the people all the words of this life, and there they shortly were found standing and teaching the people. Finally, the last verse before the episode of St Stephen tells us that every day, in the temple and *κατ' οἶκον,* they ceased not to teach and to preach Jesus as the Christ.

Ac iii 1
Ac v 12
Ac v 20
Ac v 25
Ac v 42

Hope of a National Conversion

For one other indication of the state of things during this period we must go back to St Peter's address in Solomon's porch. After denouncing in plain language the crime of the Crucifixion he declares his knowledge that both people and rulers had perpetrated it in ignorance, and he calls on these murderers of the Righteous One to repent. In other words, the doom of the old Israel was not yet sealed till not the Lord only but His faithful servants had been rejected. The leading Apostle could still cherish the hope that the nation

Ac iii 12 ff. esp *v* 17

at large might be brought to turn and bow the knee to its true Messiah. Nor, so far as appears, was there anything in St Peter's preaching to provoke plausible antagonism. Its great theme is Jesus the Messiah, crucified and raised to the right hand of God, the present object of faith, the present outpourer of spiritual gifts from above. The far-reaching consequences which might have to flow from these premisses are left for the present unexpressed.

Steps in the growth of the community

It is worth while to notice briefly the steps in the growth of the Christian community and its relations to the people at this time, so far as they are known to us. The body who return to Jerusalem after
Ac i 13 f. the Ascension are the eleven Apostles, certain women, Mary the mother of Jesus, and His brethren. Matthias is added to the Eleven in an assembly of
Ac i 15 the brethren, about 120 in number "in those days". After St Peter's discourse on the Day of Pente-
Ac ii 41 cost 3000 are added. The following time is one
Ac ii 46 f. of exultation and simplicity of heart, "praising God and having favour with *all* the people", and every day added to their number. The first collision comes on St Peter's address to the wondering multitudes after the miracle on the lame man. The
Ac iv 1–4 chief priests (*v. l.* priests), the captain of the temple and the Sadducees come upon the Apostles and imprison them; but of the hearers about 5000 are converted. Then follows the hearing before

the rulers and elders and scribes (four names being given and "all that were of high priestly family"), Ac iv 5, 6
and the Apostles are released with a warning, for Ac iv 16–21
fear of the people. Their report to the brethren Ac iv 23–31
and solemn prayer give special force to this recognition of the beginning of persecution. Then follows the story of Ananias and Sapphira. The popularity continues and multitudes of men and women join, but there is some holding off of out- Ac v 13, 14
siders. Meanwhile the cities round Jerusalem send their sick to be healed. Once more the high priest and his Sadducee friends intervene to imprison the Ac v 17 f.
Apostles. Released by an angel, they are again found teaching in the temple, and again brought before the Sanhedrin and "all the senate of the sons Ac v 21
of Israel". The incipient purpose of slaying them is stopped by Gamaliel. The result is a compromise. They are scourged and again discharged with a caution, to which again they give no heed. Their evangelic teaching continues in temple and houses alike. It is at this point that the preaching of St Stephen opens new horizons, and leads to a new course of events.

St Stephen

The Date

How long an interval had passed since the Ascension, is hard to determine, and very different views have been taken. There are however some safe limits. The accession of Festus to office in place of Felix took place in, or nearly in, A.D. 60, and the indications supplied by the Acts and Gal. i. ii. carry us back from that year to A.D. 35 or 36 as the probable date of St Paul's conversion, which apparently took place shortly after Stephen's death. At the other end of the interval the date of the Crucifixion is still uncertain, but must at all events have been early enough to leave at least three or four years before St Stephen's death: the few incidents recorded in Acts i.—v. must not therefore be taken as anything like a complete history of what was probably the quiet growth of the Church at Jerusalem.

Who were the Hellenists? Ac vi 1 ff.

The first new fact which meets us is the division of the Church at Jerusalem into a Hebrew and a Hellenistic portion. The meaning of the term Hellenist was a matter of conjecture in Chrysostom's day, and so it is still. But it is fixed with reasonable certainty, by the meaning of Ἑλληνίζω, to be simply a Greek-speaking Jew. It must therefore on no account be confused with a proselyte, though possibly a proselyte might also be called a Hellenist with reference to his language. Evidently there was no lack of spiritual energy in the Hellenistic section of the community, and it was from this section that the impulse was to proceed which was to lead to the first important changes in the primitive Judaic, I do not say Judaistic, character of the Church.

We are not told of the proportion between the two elements, but evidently both were considerable. The complaint made by the Hellenists suggests that the Hebrew Christians looked on their Hellenist brethren as having only a secondary claim on their care when the increasing numbers of the disciples rendered the eleemosynary arrangements of the community more difficult to work. We have thus here a forewarning of the troubles afterwards to arise in respect of the treatment of Gentile Christians. The Apostles recognise the need of organisation to meet the difficulty, and call on the community to provide seven men *πλήρεις πνεύματος καὶ σοφίας*, whom they themselves would set over this business, which they did by laying on of hands. It has been often noticed that all the names were Greek, which affords some presumption that all the seven, including Stephen, were Hellenists. As the last of the seven, Nicolaus, is called a proselyte of Antioch, it is probable that the others were not proselytes. Stephen was apparently already marked out as one full of faith *καὶ πνεύματος ἁγίου*.

Jealousy of Hellenists

Then comes a fresh statement of the growth of the Church. The former statement as to the growing numbers of Christians is repeated more emphatically than before with the remarkable addition that a great multitude of the priests "hearkened to the faith", i.e. (probably) no longer believed secretly only Ac vi 7
but obeyed the call of their faith by an open profession.

The opposition to Stephen

What we are told of the miracles wrought by Stephen, and of the preaching which was confirmed by these, had probably nothing to do with his office as one of the Seven. He simply exercised after his appointment the gifts which had distin-
Ac vi 9 guished him before it. He was resisted by certain men, described in a long compound phrase, which has been supposed to mean that they came from two or else from five synagogues in Jerusalem. The existence of synagogues called by these names would not be improbable in itself, but the Greek, though not smooth and correct on any interpretation, suggests only the one synagogue of the Libertines, probably freedmen of Rome, and the other names simply as descriptive of origin. They are, from the South, Cyrene and Alexandria, from the North, Cilicia and Proconsular Asia. It is natural to suppose that prominent among the Cilician antagonists would be St Paul. It is remarkable that the opposition here mentioned came not from Hebrews but from Jews of the Dispersion, though they in their turn stirred
Ac vi 12 up against Stephen the people and the elders and the scribes; and all alike were responsible for his death. As we shall see presently, it was with
Ac ix 29 the Hellenists alone that St Paul is described as coming into conflict at Jerusalem at his first visit there after his conversion. These men, probably old associates of Stephen before his conversion, found
Ac vi 10 themselves overborne by the wisdom and the spirit

with which he spoke. They therefore suborned witnesses to attest his having spoken blasphemous words against Moses and God (i.e. with having vilified the Law). He spoke unceasingly, they said, against the holy place and the Law, declaring that Jesus would destroy (*καταλύσει*) the temple and change the customs left by Moses.

To these charges Stephen's discourse is an indirect answer. What he had actually said we cannot tell with certainty. Doubtless, as in our Lord's case, there was distortion of real words. It is probable enough that Stephen saw that sooner or later the process of fulfilment of the Law in the spirit must involve its becoming obsolete in the letter, and that the conception of worship involved in this fulfilment must render unmeaning the exclusive sanctity of the temple. But his defence does not suggest that he uttered any such prediction, which indeed, as far as we can see, would have been an unprofitable act of defiance; while it is likely enough that he did plainly set forth a higher authority than that of the Law, a truer sanctity than that of the temple. His defence is in the main a vindication of himself on these lines, chiefly by indicating the anticipations of similar teaching to be found in the events of sacred history and laid down by the prophets, and on the other hand the anticipations which they likewise contained of the present Jewish unbelief. The starting-point is Abraham and his departure from Mesopotamia for a

Stephen's defence Ac vii

cf. Jn iv 21

Ac vii 2 ff. cf. Heb xi 8

land which God was to shew him,—a true parallel of the position taken up by the accused Christian Jews.
Ac vii 20 ff. Further on he speaks at great length of Moses, the forerunner of Christ, dwelling especially on the rejection of him as a self-made ruler and judge in contrast to his actual mission by God as a ruler and a redeemer: and dwelling again on his having received living oracles to give to the Jews; but all in vain, since they refused to obey them, and turned back in their hearts unto Egypt. Then he points out how
Ac vii 44 ff. till the days of David their fathers had not had the temple, but the tabernacle made by Moses from a Divine pattern, the temple being built at last only at the king's desire. There is here no condemnation of the building of the temple, as some have supposed, but there is a suggestion that its holiness was really derived from what it inherited from its predecessor,
cf. Heb viii 5 the tabernacle, a Divine pattern still abiding; that it was in fact merely one mutable phase in the manifestation of God's dwelling among men; while he quotes Is. lxvi. 1 f. to shew that God cannot dwell in any human building in the exclusive sense assumed
Ac vii 51 by the Jews. He ends with a rebuke in biblical language, pointing out that the stiffneckedness and
Is lxiii 10 hardness of heart rebuked in their fathers was repeated in them, both alike setting themselves against the Holy Spirit. He foreshadows his already clearly
Mt xxiii 34 anticipated doom by speaking, as Christ had done, of the slaying of the prophets. The last words are

not a rejection of the Law but a rebuke to the Jews for not keeping it. When he declared his vision of the Son of Man standing at the right hand of God, they drove him out of the city, and there, without the camp, as the Epistle to the Hebrews says of Christ Himself, they stoned him. Heb xiii 11

The Extension of the Church

The varied issues of that day were the beginning of the end for the Law and the Temple. Words of such far-reaching purport, carefully guarded as they had been from denunciation of any present sanctity, could not but make a deep impression, more especially when spoken by an eloquent and zealous Hellenist who had suffered martyrdom for uttering them. But further the young man Saul was present and consenting, and for him the sights and sounds were not to be in vain. And thirdly, the general persecution which ensued drove all except the Apostles from the city, scattering them over Judea and Samaria. How the Apostles were able to stay and yet escape destruction, we know not. To the stay itself they may have held themselves to be pledged if no clear intimation from above came to them to bid them leave their primary work in the city. *The results of Stephen's death* Ac viii 1 f.

Two short narratives that follow exhibit some of *The Gospel at Samaria*

Ac viii 4–25 the immediate results of that scattering. Philip, the second on the list of the Seven, preaches at Samaria and has Simon Magus for one of his converts. The Apostles, though they had not originated this preaching, recognise its results, and send down Peter and John, who pray for the bestowal of the Spirit, with its wondrous signs, upon the converts, and the prayer is granted. On their way back to Jerusalem they themselves carry on the work, preaching in many Samaritan villages. Thus, while the barriers between
Mt x 5 Jew and Samaritan recognised by our Lord had been for a while maintained, they were now deliberately let go, and this peculiar semi-Jewish people was placed within the Church on the same footing as the purest Hebrew Jews.

Baptism of the eunuch Ac viii 26–40

Again Philip is divinely guided to meet, instruct, and baptize the Ethiopian eunuch of Candace's court, a member of another race, apparently one of the God-fearers, as they were called, followers of the less distinctive parts of Jewish religion. He is then carried away to Azotus, and thence traverses all the

The seaboard of Palestine

towns of the coast northwards till he reaches Cæsarea, preaching all the way. Cæsarea, you will remember, was the political capital of Palestine at this time, and a place of great importance. Here then another great step is taken. We are still within the ancient limits of the Holy Land. But in the Apostolic age these cities of the coast were much more Greek than Jewish. At the same time there is no evidence that

Philip's preaching was addressed to others than Jews, whether Hebrews or Hellenists.

The conversion of St Paul

Ac ix

Momentous as were the consequences of St Paul's conversion for the future part of our subject, its details do not concern us now, beyond the fact that there were already Christians at Damascus. In St Luke's own record St Paul's sphere is defined by the Lord speaking to Hananiah as "to bear my name before [τῶν] ἐθνῶν τε καὶ βασιλέων υἱῶν τε Ἰσραήλ"; where it is to be observed that the sons of Israel are added as an appendix at the end, and that not only nations but kings are mentioned. In St Paul's own accounts we have, "Thou shalt be a witness to Him πρὸς πάντας ἀνθρώπους" and "delivering thee from the people and from the nations; unto whom [apparently the nations by what follows] I send thee to open their eyes, that they may turn from darkness to light, and from the power of Satan unto God, that they may receive remission of sins and an inheritance among them that are sanctified by faith in Me." But it is noteworthy that as soon as St Paul began an active Christian ministry, (i.e. apparently as soon as he had returned to Damascus from that visit to Arabia mentioned by himself, Gal. i. 17, though passed over by St Luke,) he did not depart from the line of conduct followed by the other Apostles, of speaking to the Jews first. It was in the

Ac ix 15
cf. Mt x 18
Mk xiii 9
Lk xxi 12
cf. xii 11
Ac iv 26
=Ps ii 2
Ac xxii 15
Ac xxvi 17 f.

synagogues of Damascus that his preaching as a Christian began (ix. 20): they were *Jews* whom he confounded by his discourses at Damascus (ix. 22), thus early provoking their deadly enmity.

His visit to Jerusalem

For his first visit to Jerusalem as a Christian, three years after his conversion, we have to compare the accounts[1] in Acts ix. 26—30 and Gal. i. 18—20. He went up *ἱστορῆσαι* Κηφᾶν, to 'explore' St Peter, to find out how he would be disposed to treat the persecutor now become a champion. Barnabas, who as a Cyprian may have known him in the neighbouring Tarsus, and who must have stood high with the Apostles who gave him
Ac iv 36 his significant name, introduced him to St Peter, with whom he stayed fifteen days, during which he also saw James the Lord's brother. At this time he boldly shewed himself in public as a Christian champion, disputing with the Hellenists, i.e. doubtless with those of them who had already taken the lead in the proceedings against Stephen. On their attempting to kill him, he was conveyed away by the brethren and went home to Tarsus, where he remains out of sight for some time. St Luke closes this piece of narrative with the fact that
Ac ix 31 through all Judea, Galilee, and (now) Samaria the Church had peace (i.e. for some reason persecution had ceased), and went forward in quiet growth and enlargement.

[1] See Lightfoot, *Gal.* 91 f.

Cornelius

We now come almost immediately to an incident even more decisive in its results than Stephen's death. The Apostles evidently now took the whole land, and not merely Jerusalem, as their sphere of work. There were Christians at Lydda, and there Peter went to visit them, and his presence and miracles caused fresh conversions in the whole Sharon; and the same thing happens at Joppa by the sea-coast, to which he was led on. Then comes the story of Cornelius, the Roman centurion of Cæsarea, who enjoyed the respect of all the Jews. At the hour of prayer Peter sees the thrice repeated vision of the sheet full of all manner of living things and hears the voice pronouncing that God had cleansed what he supposed to be profane. Then come in the messengers from Cornelius relating *his* vision; Peter accepts the one vision as interpreting for him the other, and "opening his mouth" (the words always have special force) declares his perception that God is no respecter of persons, but in every nation he that feareth Him and worketh righteousness is acceptable to Him. He then repeats afresh the Gospel as declared in the first instance to the Sons of Israel; and is on the other hand in the act of citing the prophets as testifying remission of sins through Messiah's name to *πάντα τὸν πιστεύοντα εἰς αὐτόν*, when the wondrous tongues are heard as a sign of the descent of the Holy Spirit on the hearers, and *οἱ*

The baptism of a proselyte

Ac ix 35

Ac ix 36 ff

Ac x 1 ff.

Ac x 9 ff.

Ac x 17 ff.

Ac x 34 f.

Ac x 36 ff.

Ac x 43 f.

Ac x 45 ἐκ περιτομῆς πιστοὶ who had accompanied Peter, at once recognise the sanction given from heaven to the reception of Gentiles, though as yet only Gentiles already associated with Judaism in faith and partly in practice. St Peter accordingly seals the acknowledgment by bestowing baptism.

ratified at Jerusalem Ac xi 1 ff. Thus far the act was his alone, though it was that of the foremost Apostle. The tidings soon reached Jerusalem and did not please all there. Circumcised Christians complained of Peter for sitting at meat with men that were uncircumcised. In reply he briefly told the whole story, appealing specially to our Lord's words about baptism with the Holy Spirit in connexion with the visible manifestation of the Spirit as fallen on those Gentiles. And this Ac xi 18 explanation satisfied the objectors, who joined in glorifying God for having given the Gentiles as well as themselves the repentance unto life.

The Preaching to the Hellenists at Antioch

The evangelisation of Antioch The scene now changes to Antioch, still in Syria, but far beyond any limits of the Holy Land. To this point, and to the neighbouring Cyprus, the fugitives from the persecution following Stephen's death had penetrated along the Phœnician seaboard. Ac xi 19 They preached as they went, but, we are told, they spoke the word to no one save only to Jews. "But

there were some of them", St Luke goes on, "men of Ac xi 20
Cyprus and Cyrene, who when they were come to
Antioch, spake unto the Hellenists also, preaching
glad tidings of the Lord Jesus". It is a common
fashion here to read 'Greeks' for 'Hellenists', with a *'Greeks' or*
few MSS., *not* including the best. It is practically *'Hellen-*
assumed that we have here a sharp antithesis between *ists'?*
Jews in the most comprehensive sense and mere
heathens. If this, however, were the case, we should
expect much more significant language to accompany
the statement, and the solemn *turning* of Paul and Ac xiii 46
Barnabas to the Gentiles at Antioch of Pisidia
would be robbed of much of its meaning. More than
one explanation of the words is possible. It is at
least curious that ἐλάλουν καὶ πρὸς τοὺς Ἑλληνιστάς Ac xi 20
resembles so closely the phrase describing St Paul's
controversial preaching at Jerusalem, ἐλάλει τε Ac ix 29
καὶ συνεζήτει πρὸς τοὺς Ἑλληνιστάς, where πρός
must have an adversative sense. So too it might
well be here "spake *against* the Hellenists", if
antagonists were found among the Hellenists at
Antioch as well as at Jerusalem. But the absence
of any further indication of opposition on their part
renders this less likely than other explanations. It
is again possible that the Hellenists are included in
the Ἰουδαῖοι, but had also a separate organisation, Ac xi 19
and that what is meant is, so to speak, a special
mission to them by Cyprians and Cyrenians, them-
selves Hellenists, as part of the general evangelisation.

But more probably Ἰουδαῖος is meant in the narrower sense of Jews proper, such as are called Ἑβραῖοι in vi. 1 (a word not used elsewhere in Acts). This, or some similarly limited sense, is the only natural sense of Ἰουδαῖοι in xiv. 1, xviii. 4, where the associated Ἕλληνες cannot be heathens, being frequenters of synagogues. Doubtless then the persons generally addressed at Antioch, and on the way there, were Hebrews, while the Cyprians and Cyrenians went further and addressed Hellenists, perhaps including the fearers of God or proselytes of the less strict sort (wrongly called 'proselytes of the gate' in modern books), such as Cornelius and probably the eunuch had been: but no one as yet preached to men entirely heathens.

Barnabas at Antioch

Both the preaching and the conversions that followed were reported to the Church at Jerusalem, Ac xi 22 ff. and Barnabas being sent down to inspect was entirely satisfied, and went to Tarsus to fetch Saul, evidently seeing that a work specially suited to him was now begun. In truth, though heathens were not yet addressed, the step taken was a great one. The Gospel was now established in a great capital beyond Palestine, surrounded by heathens, a specially important centre of the Dispersion. And now first it Ac xi 26 was that the disciples were called Christians, a name apparently given them by others.

LECTURE IV

The Church of Antioch

THE principal work of the Church of Jerusalem was now done. Henceforward we hear of it only incidentally, in so far as it had an influence on the expanding Church beyond Palestine. The transition is formed by a mission of Barnabas and Saul from Antioch to Jerusalem to carry a contribution to the brethren of Judea who were suffering from famine. This visit of St Paul to Jerusalem is passed over in his own recital in Galatians, but a sufficient explanation is given by Dr Lightfoot, and is indeed suggested by the structure of the narrative in Acts. *The contribution from Antioch* Ac xi 29 f. Lightfoot, *Gal.* p. 126

At the same time, doubtless before Barnabas and Saul arrived, a new form of persecution broke out. This time it came neither from people, nor from priests, nor scribes, nor elders, but from the king, from Herod. He slew James the son of Zebedee and imprisoned Peter, who was released by an angel, and withdrew, apparently for a time only, to another place. *Herod's prosecution* Ac xii 2 Ac xii 17

James the Lord's brother The death of James probably led to the substitution of James the Lord's brother in his place. He has not been named in the Acts till now, when he Ac xii 17 suddenly appears as the person to whom, in conjunction with the brethren, Peter sends the message with the account of his delivery from prison. From this time forward he is apparently the head of the Church of Jerusalem, and thus assumes a position of great interest in relation to our subject. It seems to me by no means improbable that he was counted henceforward as one of the Twelve in place of his namesake. But this is not at all certain.

The significance of the mission If Barnabas and Saul arrived at Jerusalem early in the persecution, it might easily happen that Saul would have no opportunity of speaking to either Peter or any other of the Twelve, for it must have been a time of confusion and probably of scattering. But the mission was accomplished: Church greeted Church with substantial tokens of Ac xii 25 brotherhood and communion, and the envoys returned to Antioch. It was no mere charitable act that they had been performing. It was the practical exhibition of fellowship with the Church of Jerusalem on the part of the young and probably to a great extent Hellenistic Church of Antioch, a recognition of the mother city by the Christians of the Jewish Dispersion, analogous to the half shekel which came from Jews scattered in all lands for the support of the temple service.

St Paul's first Missionary Journey

Antioch undertakes the work of evangelisation

After this mission of brotherhood from the Church of Antioch to that of Jerusalem in the persons of Paul and Barnabas, the first missionary journey formally and officially undertaken begins. How St Paul occupied himself during the long interval which he had spent in Cilicia, we learn neither from himself nor (Gal i 21) from St Luke. The last two verses of Gal. i. evidently refer not merely to the time just described but to the whole time between St Paul's conversion and the visit to Jerusalem described in Gal. ii., and thus are too gen- (Gal ii) eral to be evidence on this point. It is not likely however that St Paul would refrain from preaching to his own countrymen: but if he did so preach, it was as an individual, and such preaching was not part of the Apostolic work properly so called which is narrated in the Acts. On the other hand the first missionary journey of Paul and Barnabas is begun under circumstances of peculiar solemnity. Five prophets and (Ac xiii 1 ff.) teachers are named as at this time in the Church of Antioch. While the Church is engaged in worship the Holy Spirit, doubtless speaking through a prophet, bids the Church set apart Barnabas and Saul, the first and the last on the list, for the work to which 'I have called them'. With fasting, prayers and laying on of hands they are then set on their way. Thus they received a twofold authority, that of the Divine intimation, and that of the human recognition and, as it were, sealing. During this journey, and this alone, Ac xiv 4, 14 they are called by St Luke 'apostles,' i.e. envoys, not of Jesus Christ as the Twelve were and as St Paul independently was, but envoys of the Church of Antioch. This language is precisely similar to that used by St Paul respecting certain brethren when he 2 Cor viii 23 calls them ἀπόστολοι ἐκκλησιῶν. After this journey and the ratification which followed at Jerusalem, there was no need to emphasise the authoritative commission. For *this* occasion it *was* needful to lay stress on the Divine sanction given to the independent action of the Church of Antioch.

Turning to the Gentiles

On the journey Paul and Barnabas keep on the old lines as long as they are allowed. In Cyprus Ac xiii 5 they preach only in synagogues of the Jews. So it Ac xiii 14 is at first at the Pisidian Antioch. But on the second Sabbath, when nearly all the city is gathered together Ac xiii 44 ff. to hear their preaching, the Jews set themselves in opposition, and then Paul and Barnabas wax bold and say "To you it was necessary that the Word of God should first be spoken: since ye thrust it from you and judge yourselves not worthy of the eternal life, behold we turn to the Gentiles: for so hath the Lord commanded us, I have set thee for a light of the Gentiles, that thou shouldst be for salvation unto the Ac xiii 48 uttermost part of the earth". The Gentiles hearing these words rejoice, and many believe, and the Word of the Lord spreads through all that region. This incident in the synagogue at Pisidian Antioch is the true turning point at which a Gentile Christianity formally and definitely begins, and so a Judaistic Christianity becomes possible. The year was either A.D. 50 or thereabouts. Persecution followed, the Jews stirring up the chief men of the city, apparently through ladies, Ac xiii 50 probably of their own families, who hung on to the Jewish community as God-fearers. The same order of things recurs at Iconium, where again the Jewish syna- Ac xiv 1 gogue is first visited: whether it was the same at other places, we are not told. Finally the envoys on their return to Antioch assemble the Church, and tell them how "God had opened to the Gentiles a door of Ac xiv 27 faith". There they stayed "no small time". Ac xiv 28

The Conference at Jerusalem

Disquiet at Jerusalem

News of such momentous events could not fail to reach Jerusalem before long, and there much disquiet arose. Gentiles had been admitted on a large scale as members of Christian communities without circumcision, and apparently the Church of Antioch, or at least a large part of it, accepted and ratified this policy. If such a state of things were tolerated, a new conception of what it was to be a Christian would be established, and many accustomed ways of thought and action would lose their justification. It is not surprising that, as we read, certain men came down from Judea and taught the brethren, "If ye be Ac xv 1 not circumcised after the custom of Moses, ye cannot be saved". Much controversy ensuing, they commission Paul and Barnabas with others of their number to go up to the Apostles and elders at Jerusalem on this question. It may be that St Paul had at first hesitated, for he says he went up by revelation. From himself we receive, according to the best explanation, the account of the confidential conferences with the leading people behind the scenes; from St Luke, the account of the larger assembly at which the results so arranged were formally ratified.

Ac xv 2

Gal ii 2

Ac xv 4 ff.

St Paul and the Three

Gal ii 2

To the original Apostles, or the chief of them, St Paul communicated what he calls 'The gospel which he preached among the Gentiles', explaining i.e. the principles on which he acted in admitting Gentiles to Christian fellowship; his position towards them in the matter was a peculiar one, as we may see by the restraints which he felt in writing to the Galatians. On the one hand he asked from them no authority, as though they had a right to decide the matter against him: on the other he felt that a difference between him and them on such a matter would involve a fatal schism between Gentile and Judean Christianity—"lest I should be running or had already been running in vain". This feeling was in fact the same as that which made him lay so much stress on the acceptance of the Gentile offering by the Judean Churches at the end of the Epistle to the Romans.

Gal ii 2

Rom xv 25 ff.

Towards the aggressive Jewish Christians on the other hand, "the intruded false brethren" as he calls them, i.e. intruded into the Church of Antioch, a sphere which did not concern them, he used very different conduct. He refused to let Titus, who had come with him from Antioch, be circumcised, as they demanded, and as even the Jerusalem Apostles apparently suggested his doing for the sake of easing difficulties. Such at least—in both respects (non-circumcision and Apostolic advice) is Lightfoot's very probable interpretation. Some years ago I was inclined to think that what St Paul denies was not Titus's circumcision, but his compulsory circumcision. The words will bear this meaning: but it does not fit so well into the context or into St Paul's singularly careful and circumspect policy. To the Apostles themselves, when this was their advice, he would not yield even for an hour. But he did not thereby forfeit the support of James, Peter and John. They recognised St Paul's Divine commission to an independent Apostleship of the Gentiles and the grace of God which had attested it, and gave them right hands of fellowship on these terms of different spheres; only begging them to keep the poor of Judea in mind, 'a thing', says St Paul (for this the words really mean) 'which I also made it a point for this very reason to do';—how sedulously, his later words and acts attest.

Was Titus circumcised? Gal ii 4

Gal ii 3

App to N. T. on Gal ii 5

Terms of agreement

Gal ii 9

Gal ii 10

The Decision of the Conference

The public conference Ac xv 6 ff. We need not go into the details of the larger assembly when the apostles and elders met together: indeed we know nothing of the long discussion (πολλῆς ζητήσεως), only of Peter's speech, the narrative of Barnabas and Paul, and James's final speech, in which he ended by giving his opinion in favour of not troubling converts from the Gentiles, but enjoining Ac xv 20 on them four special abstinences; from food offered to idols, fornication, things strangled, and blood. This Ac xv 22 ff. was accepted by the whole Church, and a letter written to this effect in the name of the apostles and elder brethren, disclaiming the intrusive brethren, and speaking warmly of Barnabas and Paul.

The special prohibitions not 'Noachid' This important decision is obscure in some points. The negative aspect of it is clear enough, and speaks volumes. Not only circumcision disappears, but the Sabbath and all other sacred seasons, distinctions of clean and unclean meats with special exceptions, and the Levitical legislation generally: nor again is anything said about the Ten Commandments. On what ground were these four particular abstinences prescribed? It will not be wasting time to consider this question, though it must be very briefly. A very plausible view, widely held since the seventeenth century, when Christian scholars began to study post-biblical Jewish literature in earnest, is that they represent what the later Jews called the Seven Commandments of the Sons of Noah, ideally ordained by God for the non-Jewish descendants of Noah. It was held[1] that these seven precepts were binding on every *Gêr Tôshav*, or stranger sojourning in the land of Israel, and modern critics have without any evidence assumed the identity of a *Gêr Tôshav* with a σεβόμενος, and inferred that the purpose of the Jerusalem decision was to admit Gentiles on the footing of σεβόμενοι. This would be in fact making them a kind of associates, not full members, of the Christian Community. If this was to be their position, while Jewish Christians stood on a different footing, none but Jews could be Christians in the fullest sense. But apart from the want of evidence for any connexion between the σεβόμενοι and the Noachid Commandments, the coincidence between these Commandments and the Jerusalem precepts is very imperfect. They are in fact applications of five or six of the Ten Commandments (the 1st, 4th, 9th, and 10th and perhaps the 5th being omitted), with one or perhaps two additions. They are 1, against profanation of God's Name (III); 2, against idolatry (II); 3, against fornication or perhaps incest (the phrase is ambiguous) (VII); 4, against murder (VI); 5, against theft (VIII); 6, enjoins respect for judges, i.e. civil authority; perhaps an application of V. These six were said to have been given to Adam, a 7th being added and given to Noah, against "a piece from the

[1] Schürer II. ii. 318 Eng. Tr.

living" i.e. the live ox or other animal, one form of the prohibition of eating blood. Now at least three of the four Jerusalem precepts, and perhaps all four, have something answering to them in these seven Noachid Commandments, but the correspondence is not exact, and at all events four are absent. So that identification would be very difficult even if we had any reason to believe these rabbinical Commandments to have been formally imposed on the σεβόμενοι.

nor 'Levitical' This difficulty has led of late to an inclination to trace the Jerusalem precepts rather to those Levitical injunctions which the Pentateuch itself makes binding on strangers or sojourners. Here however the want of correspondence is still greater; and if the written letter of the Law was to furnish the precepts, the variation from them in both matter and number would be inexplicable.

nor 'casual' Another suggestion is that the precepts answer to points which happened to be put forward by scrupulously minded Jewish Christians, and which the Apostles thought might be conceded without breach of principle. This is of course possible, and it supersedes the necessity of trying to explain the selection; but it does not seem to me to tally naturally with the language actually used in the Epistle to Antioch. Ac xv 28

nor even concessions to Judaic spirit All these three explanations take for granted that the four precepts are simply concessions to the Judaic side. It seems more natural however to suppose that they were meant as concrete indications of pure and true religion, not of Judaism in the exclusive sense. There was a real risk that Gentile converts admitted freely into full communion without having to submit to a painful and in many eyes disgraceful rite, as Jewish proselytes had, might misinterpret and misuse their liberty, just as we see afterwards at Corinth. There was much to be said for laying this emphatic stress on certain well chosen abstinences or restraints held to have a close connexion with purity of religion, and they were none the worse for being coincident with hallowed Jewish laws or traditions, though this was not the source of their authority. It was a clear gain that their agreement with the inherited moral associations of Jews should make the whole arrangement more acceptable to the Jewish party in the Church, since they were not of a nature to suggest any kind of obligation on Gentile converts to obey any part of the Mosaic Law. They were no doubt biblical, but they were of pre-Mosaic origin[1].

Idolatry and uncleanness

Three of the four answer to three great mysteries of human life or experience, and to three corresponding forms of reverence. Two of these are obvious. It is by no fanciful or accidental association that idolatry and uncleanness stand so often together. Apart from the familiar association of impure rites with certain forms of idolatrous worship, (a connexion on which too much stress ought not in fairness to be

[1] Cf. Aug. c. Faust. 32, 13. See Appendix.

laid, considering how many forms of idolatry were and are free from that particular stain), both are profanations as well as disloyalties. In all communion with God, in the most intimate form of communion with man, the sense of being on holy ground is the most essential condition; and to lay stress on this at the outset of a Christian profession might naturally be thought a salutary safeguard for new converts. From our present English point of view it might be urged that uncleanness and even an indirect participation in idolatry can be safely assumed to be rejected in principle by every one who claimed to be a Christian at all: but the moral atmosphere of Syria in the first century doubtless made startling combinations of moral ideas possible, if indeed we may not say that they have existed and do exist in every Christian century.

'Blood'

The precept about blood is at first sight more difficult to explain, the explanation lies, I doubt not, in the feeling of mystery entertained by various peoples of antiquity with respect to blood[1]. Abstinence from blood was in fact an outward expression of reverence for what Gen. i. 30 calls 'the living soul' in every animal of the warm-blooded races, a mysterious tabernacling of life in the lower creation, life being that element or phenomenon of the visible world which seemed the most closely akin to the Divine nature, a third mystery below the mysteries of God and of man. On the one hand this feeling

[1] Cf. Ewald, *Antiquities of Israel*, Eng. Tr. p. 37. See Appendix.

received special consecration from Jewish law and usage, on the other it was not exclusively Jewish.

Things strangled

The subject of the fourth precept, things strangled, is much harder to explain. There is, I believe, no evidence of any exactly corresponding usage either in the first or in any earlier century, though the passage in Acts naturally had some influence on Christian practice in later times. The attempts to find it in the Pentateuch (e.g. Lev. xvii. 13) quite fail. It is on the other hand very conceivable that the flesh of strangled animals, not having the blood let out when they were killed, would be counted unlawful food by the Jews[1], though strange to say we nowhere read that it actually was so. The difficulty is that in that case we should have a separate fourth precept referring only to a particular case of the third precept. This difficulty remains the same, however we understand the intention of the precepts as a whole. It must I fear at present be left unsolved. It was very early found so perplexing that the "Western" text omitted the words in both places.

These precepts analogous to baptismal renunciations

Two or three general remarks must be made before we leave the subject. First, these substitutes for circumcision were intrinsically by no means *ejusdem generis*. That was a physical operation which could be absolutely enforced before admission to fellowship, and which then in the natural course of

[1] Cf. Orig. c. Cels. viii. 30. See Appendix.

things remained permanently. The four precepts were precepts only. As conditions they could be imposed in the form of *promises* only, and would thus answer to the renunciations which early became a condition of baptism. But even this much was
Ac xv 20 perhaps not enforced, for we read only of "enjoining",
Ac xv 28 and of "not laying on a burden", ending with the
Ac xv 29 assurance "from which things if ye keep yourselves, it shall be well with you" (εὖ πράξετε).

and limited in address

Again the precepts were not addressed, as is often assumed, to all heathens whom St Paul or others might at any time convert, but very definitely to the
Ac xv 23 brethren that were in Antioch and Syria and Cilicia. Nor must it be supposed that the mention of Cilicia carries us into an altogether new region, which might be supposed to represent the rest of what we call Asia Minor. At this time Cilicia was practically part of Syria, as indeed other passages of the New Testament indirectly bear witness. Further the mention of Antioch as well as Syria, of which it was the capital, shews that it was the special destination of the epistle, though scattered congregations of Syria and Cilicia were likewise addressed by it. But no account was taken of future converts in other more distant lands. It was a local determination for a special emergency.

Later traces of the Epistles in the Acts

This being the case, we need not, thirdly, be surprised that it left such faint traces behind. We read indeed that Paul and Silas in going through the cities in the region of Derbe and Lystra "delivered them the decrees for to keep, which had been ordained of the apostles and elders that were at Jerusalem." In other words, on the first missionary journey after the Jerusalem conference they loyally gave currency to the precepts in a region which, though not within the address of the epistle, had been already visited by them when it was written, and which they were now visiting a second time to stablish the infant congregations. But St Luke is silent about any similar proceeding in the new regions to which they then penetrated, and in all subsequent journeys. Again St James and the elders at Jerusalem make allusion to the precepts, but that is a different matter. The silence is not conclusive evidence: but we might reasonably have expected to find some traces of the precepts somewhere, had St Paul continued to promulgate them. In his epistles St Paul himself is wholly silent on the subject. This would be strange as regards his account of the visit to Jerusalem in Gal. ii., were it not that he is describing that visit solely from the point of view of his own relation to the Twelve and with reference to the failure to enforce circumcision: and there was no real reason why he should confuse his very rapid sketch by a reference to a measure the importance of which had probably long already passed away. The difference which some insist on between the absolute prohibition of εἰδω-

Ac xvi 4

Ac xxi 25

but not in Pauline Epistles

λόθυτα in the Jerusalem precept and Paul's much more guarded directions in 1 Cor. is just the difference between a broad rule laid down antecedently for general practice and the discrimination in its application which a wise spiritual guide, eager to lead his disciples behind the rule to the principle, would naturally inculcate on his disciples when cases of conscience had already arisen. The precepts about blood and things strangled, however sound in principle, may easily have been found liable to do more harm than good in practice, and so have been let fall by St Paul.

1 Cor viii –x

St Peter at Antioch

St Peter rebuked by St Paul

A remarkable sequel to the decision of the Jerusalem conference is the incident at Antioch briefly described in Gal. ii. 11—14. Apparently the return of Paul and Barnabas from Jerusalem with Judas and Silas had been followed pretty soon by a visit from St Peter to Antioch. Nothing was more natural than that he should be anxious to lose little time before making personal acquaintance with the vigorous young community which had just received such emphatic recognition. On his arrival he joined, as others did, in sitting at table with uncircumcised converts, just as we saw him doing spontaneously at Cæsarea a long time before. When however "certain" came down from James, he withdrew

Ac xi 3

Gal ii 12

himself from this public converse with Gentile converts, for fear of giving offence to these men, who were circumcised Christians of Jerusalem. Not only this: his example and perhaps advice induced "the rest of the Jews", St Paul says, i.e. among the converts, to do the same, including even Barnabas. St Paul stood alone apparently, and found himself compelled to rebuke Peter publicly for his dissimulation in thus shewing practical disloyalty to the principles which, when all seemed prospering, he not only had accepted, but had just been putting into practice. Gal ii 13

St Peter's policy due to no antagonism in principle

Thus a new crisis had suddenly arisen. If St Peter's present policy were continued, St Paul saw that the Gentile converts would feel that they had been admitted under false pretences, and "the truth of the Gospel", as St Paul significantly calls it, would be gravely imperilled. It is astonishing that any one should ever have thought this passage evidence of antagonism in principle between the two Apostles, though no doubt the proportion of conviction as to the force of different claims to authority was not identical. What St Paul rebuked was not a doctrinal but a moral aberration of St Peter: he was simply unfaithful to his own convictions. The temptation was doubtless a strong one: the whole story shews that the decision made at Jerusalem had not really satisfied a considerable party in the Church of Jerusalem. What is not so easy to understand with Gal ii 14

but to false opportunism

certainty is the ground taken up by St Peter in inducing others to follow him. It cannot have been any subtle distinction about this or that form of

Gal ii 14

intercourse, for St Paul called it broadly "a compelling of the Gentiles to Judaize". Probably it was a plea of inopportuneness: "more important to keep our Jerusalem friends in good humour than to avoid every possible risk of estranging your new Gentile converts: no need to reject them or to tell them to be circumcised, but no need either for us Jews to be publicly fraternising with them, now that we know what offence that will give at Jerusalem: better wait awhile and see whether things do not come right of themselves if only we are not in too great a hurry". Plausible reasoning this would have been, and some sort of plausible reasoning there must have been to ensnare Barnabas and indeed to delude St Peter

depriving Gentile Christians of full rights of membership

himself. But what it amounted to was that multitudes of baptized Gentile Christians, hitherto treated on terms of perfect equality, were now to be practically exhibited as unfit company for the circumcised Apostles of the Lord who died for them. Such judiciousness, St Paul might well say, was at bottom only moral cowardice; and such conduct, though in form it was not an expulsion of the Gentile converts, but only a self-withdrawal from their company, was in effect a summons to them to become Jews if they wished to remain in the fullest sense Christians. St Paul does not tell us how the dispute ended: but, as he continued on excellent terms with the Jerusalem Apostles and yet went forward with an unencumbered Gospel in his hand, it is reasonable to suppose that St Peter and the rest acknowledged him to be in the right. Otherwise the history of the Church must have taken a very different turn.

St Paul acknowledged to be right

The attitude of St James

No evidence of opposition in principle

Gal ii 12

One question remains, slightly touched upon above,—What was James's part in the matter? "Before that certain came from James", St Paul says. These words do at first sight suggest that the line followed at this time by James may be safely inferred from the line which these men took, as reflected in St Peter's conduct after their arrival. A second by no means identical inference would be that St James's habitual attitude towards Gentile Christianity may be safely inferred from the line which he followed at this time; in other words, that he did *in principle* insist that a man must become a Jew in order to become a Christian, and accordingly insisted on the universal need of circumcision. If this were true, we should have evidence here of a fundamental difference between the leaders of the Apostolic Church. As there is no other evidence whatever in the New Testament to this effect (for St Paul's language about *οἱ δοκοῦντες εἶναί τι* has manifestly reference to the kind of adverse authority which others ascribed

Gal ii 5-9

to the pillar-apostles), the point is important. For if the fact were true, we should expect some other indications of it in St Paul's epistles (waiving the Acts). But further, St Paul here places St James on exactly the same footing as St Peter, nay, places him first, as cordially accepting the mission of Barnabas and himself, and thus confirms the representations of the Acts.

Gal ii 9

yet in some way directly responsible

Gal ii 12

On the other hand, as St Paul speaks of the men as coming "from James", we cannot in fairness suppose that he meant only "from Jerusalem", which it would have been quite easy and in that case much more natural to say. Some personal relation to James must be assumed, though certainly not the meaning "some of James's party", which would have been *τινὰς τῶν ἀπὸ Ἰακώβου*. One common view, well defended by Lightfoot, is that they had a real mission from James but took a line of their own. This is certainly possible; but the language does rather suggest some direct responsibility on James's part. The *τινὲς ἐξ ἡμῶν ἐτάραξαν ὑμᾶς* of Acts xv. 24 (i.e. some of the many members of the Jerusalem Church) is not an exact parallel to *ἐλθεῖν τινὰς ἀπὸ Ἰακώβου*, a single definitely named man in authority. Nor is there the slightest reason to suppose that these men of Acts xv. 24 had any commission whatever, used or not used, from the Jerusalem authorities. This need not however imply anything more than a present policy, as distinguished from a permanent principle. If I am right in supposing that St Peter must have had a plausible defence to make which beguiled the rest and himself, it may well be that the suggestion of it came from James, and ultimately from others at Jerusalem. Uneasiness may well have been felt, after St Peter had started, about his possible conduct at Antioch, especially if his conduct at Cæsarea were remembered; a discontent at first latent may have presently come to the surface, and James may have thought it most prudent to send cautions to Peter. That St Paul does not involve him directly in the rebuke is sufficiently explained by the fact that he had not committed himself, as Peter by this time had done, by companying personally with the Gentile converts. There would thus be in his case no exhibition of ὑπόκρισις, though there might be retrogression. St Paul would be able to do full justice to difficulties in the way of a consistently comprehensive view within the horizon of Jerusalem, while it was impossible for him to extend the same indulgence to St Peter, who had come within the horizon of Antioch, and had at first acted as St Paul himself did.

and perhaps originating the pleas of opportunism

Gal ii 13

The results of the controversy

It is evident that this incident at Antioch, which at first seemed full of danger to the spread of the Gospel, must eventually have powerfully confirmed

Confirmation of the decision of the conference

the decisiveness of the letter written from Jerusalem. If the Jerusalem authorities were weak-kneed in carrying out the policy which they had accepted, and then, when resisted by St Paul, confessed him to be in the right, as apparently they must have done, they were thenceforth doubly committed to concur heartily with the character of St Paul's work.

The problem set before the Gentile church

Thus from this time forward the two sides of our Lord's teaching and action in respect of the Law were both for a while embodied in living societies of men. The fulfilment of the Law, as distinguished from the observance of its letter, was now the exclusive ideal of the Gentile Church, which in most places had doubtless in the first age a kernel of Jewish converts, and which in all ages was to rest on the old foundations of Israel and to find guidance in its Scriptures, but was henceforth not under a law but under grace. How this was to be done was a terribly difficult problem, never perhaps distinctly contemplated by any large body of Christians, and still but partially solved. But a recognition of the existence and the vital nature of the problem throws great light on the failures and the successes of which Church History is the record; and still more on the vast work which still lies before the Christian community in the future. But the crisis was not equally important for the Jewish portion of the Church. To have recognised the equal validity of a Christianity not bound by the Law could not indeed but react on

Jewish Christians not immediately affected

men's thoughts on their own relation to the Law, and on Him who was the common object of faith to Jewish and to Gentile Christians: the legal question led up to questions of the highest theology. It was a grave reminder that Stephen's teaching was either true or false; and that, if true, it could not remain inoperative for any baptized Christian. But the recognition of the Gentiles as Christians without the Law did not in itself change the position of those who had been born under the Law, or warn them to abandon at once the observances which they had hitherto followed. Till the voice of God was heard in quite other accents, a Palestinian Church could not but be more or less a Judaic Church. This temporary duality within Christendom is constantly overlooked or misunderstood: but, if we think a little on the circumstances of the case, we must see that it was inevitable. Moreover the dualism can never have been sharp and absolute, on account of the existence of the Diaspora. Little as we know in detail of the religious life of ordinary circumcised Jews of the Dispersion, it is plain that when they became Christians, their manner of life must have been intermediate between that of Palestinian Christians and Gentile Christians.

The resultant Dualism temporary

and modified by the 'Dispersion'

LECTURE V

The Independent Activity of St Paul

The circumcision of Timothy

Timothy a Jew in everything except circumcision

It was under the new and encouraging sanction afforded by the ratification of Gentile freedom at Jerusalem that what is called the second missionary journey of St Paul was undertaken. With most of its details we are not now concerned. But it is of

Ac xvi 3 special interest to note that at Lystra he caused Timothy to be circumcised. The statement has been much questioned as at variance with St Paul's conduct

Gal ii 3 as regards Titus, for which (however we understand it) we have his own authority. But in truth the difference of the two cases admirably illustrates the precise position of things. Titus was wholly a Gentile: to circumcise him would not have been to follow any principle, but merely to accept what if allowable at all would have been nothing better than a prudential concession to temporary difficulties. But what was Timothy? He was notoriously the

Ac xvi 3 son of a Gentile father: everyone would therefore know that he had not been circumcised in childhood:

the father would never have tolerated what would
have been in his eyes such a degradation as that. But
except in this physical sense Timothy was not a Gen-
tile at all. His mother was a Jewess, and this of itself Ac xvi 1
made it impossible for Jews to regard him as falling
under a rule laid down for pure Gentiles. But further,
as we learn in St Paul's letters to him, he had been
brought up by a mother with whom devout faith was 2 Tim i 5; iii 15
both personal and inherited, and from a babe had drunk
the milk of the Jewish Scriptures. Thus brought up,
he could not count either as a proselyte in the strict
sense or as a σεβόμενος. He was a Jew in every-
thing but circumcision, and what amount of exclusion
from Jewish religious observances that would involve
at this time in Lycaonia, we know not. At every
turn we are reminded at once of the enormous
distinctive historical importance of the Jewish Dis-
persion and of the exceeding slenderness of our own
knowledge of it. Having then been brought up as a *circumcised not simply as a Christian*
Jew, he had become a Christian, as well as his mother
(Ἰουδαίας πιστῆς), probably on St Paul's former visit Ac xvi 1
to Lycaonia, as may be reasonably inferred from
various allusions. It is at least clear from St Luke's
language that he had been a Christian for some time.
Was it then simply as a Christian of Jewish education
and partly Jewish birth that St Paul circumcised
him? That on this supposition he should do so was
I think neither clearly probable nor clearly impro-
bable. He might think it best that the one flaw

in Timothy's complete position as a Jew should be corrected, for fear he should seem to be taking advantage on merely technical grounds of the liberty conceded to Gentiles who became Christians. In this case the same would hold good of any other convert who had a similar family history. On the other hand St Paul might as naturally regard circumcision performed in manhood under these circumstances as merely a pedantic observance of a law that had lost its significance for one who had now for some time been a Christian convert. But the truth is that St Luke distinctly indicates the act to have arisen out of a quite special circumstance. St Paul was proposing to take Timothy with him on his missionary journey, (virtually, as it would seem, in place of Barnabas who had just separated from him,) Timothy being in high repute among the Christians in those parts; and this ministry to which St Paul was destining him was the reason for his circumcision. As a private person it might not be necessary to decide whether Timothy was to count as a Jewish or as a Gentile convert: as a missionary he must in practice choose, and the choice could not be doubtful. If by the side of the Pharisee of Tarsus he stood as a Gentile convert on the strength of being uncircumcised, he would throw away every chance of influencing Jews without any corresponding gain of Gentiles, for his true history would soon be well known. Yet if he went forth to preach as a Jew

but with a view to mission work

Ac xvi 3

Ac xv 39

without circumcision, he would scandalise the Jews even more: he would be regarded as the thin end of a Pauline wedge for casting a slight on circumcision for Jews no less than for Gentiles. If on the other hand he took the bold and striking step of submitting in manhood to an operation of such severity and a rite so significant, he was giving the most emphatic pledge possible that he claimed his place unreservedly as a child of Israel, and thereby gave fresh and striking confirmation to St Paul's perseveringly followed policy "to the Jew first and also to Rom i 16
the Greek." It matters little whether the Jews in those regions of whom St Luke speaks as the Ac xvi 3
persons on whose account St Paul did this were unbelieving or Christian Jews. The act could not but favourably impress both classes alike; while its chief importance would be for those Jews who had not yet heard the Gospel.

If this explanation be the right one, and it seems to me that which the circumstances and St Luke's language suggest, this matter of Timothy is in perfect harmony with St Paul's refusal to circumcise Titus, while it also leads naturally to that indication of loyalty to the Jerusalem precepts which we have Ac xvi 4
already had occasion to notice.

The advance into Europe

Through Phrygia and Galatia to Troas

Ac xvi 5

The next verse seems intended to shew that the work thus begun was at once prospered, "the Churches were strengthened in the faith, and increased in number daily." It would seem that St Paul's intention had been to take the great frequented road which ran westward through Lycaonia to Proconsular Asia, doubtless with the idea of striking at once at its capital, the capital of the whole peninsula, Ephesus. But this was not to be for some time to come. Under Divine guidance the missionaries took a slanting north-west course through the interior, through Phrygia and Galatia proper[1], though St Paul's words *δι' ἀσθένειαν τῆς σαρκός* seem to imply that his *preaching* there was due to a detention on account of illness. At all events this was the time when the Galatians first received the Gospel from him; and to them we shall presently have to return. Having been forbidden to enter Asia now, he seems to have aimed at Bithynia, perhaps intending to go on further east to the Pontic sea-coast. But here again his course was changed by a Divine intimation. At Alexandria Troas the vision of the man of Macedonia invited him to cross the water, and so the first apostolic mission to Europe began.

(Margin: Ac xvi 6; Gal iv 13; Ac xvi 7; Ac xvi 9)

From Philippi to Corinth

At Philippi we need notice only the preaching to

[1] See Lightfoot, *Gal.* p. 22, *Col.* pp. 24–28.

the women at the *proseucha* by the river side; evi- Ac xvi 13
dently in St Luke's intention (though Schürer[1] now thinks otherwise) a different place of worship from a synagogue, though synagogues are doubtless (as he shews) called by this name. At Thessalonica they preach in the synagogue on three sabbaths. They Ac xvii 2 ff.
convert some Jews, many *σεβόμενοι*, and not a few ladies of rank, apparently as before Jewish wives of heathen men of distinction. But the main body of the Jews stir up the heathen against them on the pretext of sedition, and they think it wiser to escape to Berœa. There they have a better reception from Ac xvii 10
the Jews till envoys come from Thessalonica, on which St Paul is again urged to depart and conducted to Athens. We are all familiar with what took place Ac xvii 16
there: there is no mention of Jews. From the literary St Paul now passes to the commercial capital of Greece proper, to Corinth, and so comes at once Ac xviii 1
among Jews again. He finds there Aquila, a Jew of Pontus, who was apparently destined to play an important part in his work afterwards. Every sabbath St Paul preaches in the synagogue, and converts both Ac xviii 4
Jews and Greeks, i.e., as we have seen, probably *σεβόμενοι*.

The Epistles to the Thessalonians

It was during the year and a half spent at Corinth that the two Epistles were written to the Thessalonian

[1] *History of Jewish People* II. ii. 69 f. Eng. Tr.

Church, that Church which he had founded on the same journey in passing through Macedonia.

Traces of Jewish opposition

1 Thess ii 14-16

The first Epistle contains one vehement passage written with keen experience after the dangers and sufferings of the last few months. It begins remarkably, after a praise of the Thessalonians for the manner in which the word of God which they had received had been carried into act in their lives, with comparing this active faith of theirs to that of the Christian Churches of Judea (*ὑμεῖς γὰρ μιμηταὶ ἐγενήθητε*), for this Gentile Church, he says, had suffered the same treatment from its own countrymen that the Christians of Judea had from the Jews, "who both killed the Lord Jesus and the prophets, and drave out us, and please not God, and are contrary to all men; forbidding us to speak to

1 Thess ii 16

the Gentiles." In this connexion the *ἀναπληρῶσαι αὐτῶν τὰς ἁμαρτίας* recalls the tremendous words of Matthew xxiii. 32, and the *πάντοτε* recalls Stephen's

Ac vii 51 f.

'Ye do always (*ἀεί*) resist.'

This outburst was certainly not without a motive. It doubtless has more to do with the greater part of the Epistle than appears at first sight. Much of it is best understood as an indirect reply to insinuations against St Paul which had been whispered into Thessalonian ears. The accusers were evidently Jews, possibly unbelievers, possibly Christian Jews of the stamp of the intrusive brethren who came to Antioch. Both classes were in different ways hostile to St Paul. But the absence of doctrinal warnings points rather to unbelieving Jews.

They too are doubtless the *ἄτοποι καὶ πονηροὶ ἄνθρωποι* of the second Epistle, from whom he would have the Thessalonians pray that he may be delivered, men who though they had inherited the worship of the one true God were yet devoid of *ἡ πίστις*, that true faith in Him which rested on the recognition of His Son. Another clear reference to them is in 2 Thess. i. 8, where the criminal ignorance of God among heathens and the criminal refusal to hearken to the Gospel of the Lord Jesus stand side by side as alike objects of God's just judgment. 2 Thess iii 2

From Corinth to Ephesus

The departure from Corinth is again due to Jewish accusations, and now St Paul decides to return to Palestine. About the vow on the completion of which he shaved his head at Cenchreæ before sailing we know nothing in detail. It was of course not the performance of an appointed ordinance, but a voluntary religious act, evidently a Jewish act, (cf. one of the forms of the Nazirite vow). It is of special interest as an indication of St Paul's personal relation to the Levitical institutions in connexion with the vow of Acts xxi. 23. Ac xviii 12 ff. *St Paul's vow* Ac xviii 18 Nu vi 9 18

He permitted himself before going on to Judea to carry out the intention with which he had left *The new centre*

Ac xviii 19 Lycaonia so far as to make an entrance, as it were, at Ephesus, and preached there in the synagogue, but apparently once only. Resisting an appeal to him to stay, but promising to return if God permitted, he took ship to Cæsarea, the scene of Cornelius's vision, went up to Jerusalem and greeted the Church there, thus joining afresh the old bonds of goodwill, and then returned to the Church which had first sent him
Ac xviii 23 forth, to Antioch. St Luke intimates that he stayed there some time, but there is no pause in the narrative. The centre of activity, formerly at Jerusalem, then at Antioch, is now about to be shifted to Ephesus, and here we find ourselves at the transition. From Antioch St Paul proceeded through the Phrygian and Galatian Churches founded on the preceding journey, in order to stablish them, as on that journey he had in like manner stablished the Lycaonian Churches, and so he reached Ephesus. There he
Ac xix 2 came in contact with a curious, immature form of Christianity, representing apparently such a faith in our Lord as belonged to the time after the Baptist's preaching, before the Crucifixion and Ascension.
Ac xviii 24 ff. Apollos had shortly before been led by Priscilla and Aquila to advance from a similar position to full Christianity, and was now preaching at Corinth according to his riper faith.

St Paul at Ephesus

These two incidents concern our subject by shewing what transitional forms of belief between mere Judaism and the faith of the Gospel were still possible, though only as survivals from an earlier time. At Ephesus St Paul preached in the synagogue for three months. But when the old spirit shewed itself among the Jews, "when some," St Luke says, "were hardened and disobedient, speaking evil of the Way before the multitude, he departed from them (ἀποστὰς ἀπ' αὐτῶν) and separated the disciples (ἀφώρισεν), reasoning daily in the σχολή or lecture-hall of Tyrannus," not improbably a building at Ephesus then known by that name. The whole statement is very instructive. At first St Paul does his best to treat the Jews as simply imperfect Christians. Their synagogue is not merely a place where he preaches, but the place where he and all the Christians of Ephesus worship. This was virtually a claim on their behalf to be the truest Israelites. But a separation, not of his making, comes at last, and he is constrained to form a separate Christian congregation, though we are not told where they met, for the σχολή of Tyrannus was apparently only the place for his public preaching, probably visited by Gentiles at least as freely as by Jews. We have however no reason to conclude that the congregation thus formed was exclusively Gentile; and this negative fact is of

Separation from the synagogue

Ac xix 9

Growth of a mixed Church

consequence, as bearing on the assumptions frequently made about sharp divisions between the two classes of converts. St Luke merely says τοὺς μαθητάς, i.e. doubtless the Christian believers, whether Jews or Gentiles. This state of things continued for two
Ac xix 10 years "so that all that dwelt in Asia heard the word of the Lord, both Jews and Gentiles." This short and quiet verse sums up a time fruitful in after results, the firm planting and spreading of the Church in Ephesus and Proconsular Asia generally. It may have included various journeyings. It may also have included dangerous conflicts, if we may apply to this
1 Cor xv 32 time the allusion to a 'fight with beasts' at Ephesus. At all events the words refer to what happened at *some* time in this long stay at Ephesus, though possibly in its later months. We may gather from his words to the Ephesian elders a few months
Ac xx 19 later that the Jews were the instigators. For the evangelisation of the empire it was not less important than the consolidation of the Church of Antioch, for Ephesus held a central position in the Greek world. Here then another great stage is reached. No such break in the Acts occurs again to the end, when Rome, the centre of the whole world, is reached at last.

Plans for the future Ac xix 21

St Paul's purpose of going to Rome is recorded in distinct language in the very next verse; but it is as clearly intimated that first he must visit Jerusalem, and before setting out for Jerusalem he must revisit

Macedonia and Achaia, evidently to stablish the Churches there, as in the case of Lycaonia first, and Phrygia and Galatia afterwards. Yet there was a difference too. In this case more than stablishing was wanted, for news had now come of disorders in the Corinthian Church. A vivid picture of this time and the following months, drawn from a combination of the Acts with the Epistles, is given by Lightfoot, *Gal.* 38 ff.

The Epistles to the Corinthians

Here come in the two Epistles to Corinthians, separated from each other by a few months. Neither in their case nor in that of other Epistles can I do more than glance at some of the more important passages bearing on our subject. Thus it would be unprofitable to discuss the controversies about the supposed party of Christ (ἐγὼ δὲ Χριστοῦ), as a Judaistic party, in i. 12. On the other hand the words ἐγὼ δὲ Κηφᾶ seem to imply that there were already some at Corinth who at least looked up to the Jerusalem Apostles in preference to St Paul. But to what lengths this partisanship went, we do not know. It is at least remarkable that the Epistle is to all appearance free from direct or indirect warnings against Judaistic limitations of the Gospel.

The 'Cephas party'

1 Cor i 12

The passage in i. 22—25 on the various ways in which the idea of a crucified Messiah gave umbrage

The Scandal of the Cross

to Jews and to Greeks respectively, is instructive as to St Paul's habit of setting the two pre-Christian lines as parallel, but not identical; and the context shews that he meant to suggest that the characteristic temptations of Jews and Gentiles still lingered on, though in a modified form, in Jewish Christians and Gentile Christians.

Christ our Passover
1 Cor v 6–8

The well-known passage on leaven and the Passover illustrates well the point of view from which St Paul writes throughout. In the midst of an anxious exhortation on serious moral disorder he makes his appeal to the idea of the Jewish Passover as in one sense authoritative for these Gentile converts, coupling them with himself in 'Christ *our* Passover' and 'Let *us* keep the feast,' while on the other hand he as clearly indicates that as an institution the Passover had no bindingness for them, having been perfectly fulfilled in Messiah's death; and on this death he founds the appeal for entire newness of life; nor is it unlikely that ἐν ζύμῃ παλαιᾷ was meant to include Jewish as well as Gentile leaven.

Circumcision and uncircumcision
1 Cor vii 17–24

One passage in c. vii. deserves special attention. It is often taken, quite erroneously, as part of the discussion on marriage which occupies the rest of the chapter. It is really a digression to a much wider principle, laid down both for its own sake and for the sake of the special application to marriage which suggests the exposition. Among the examples of a

man remaining before God in that state *in* which 1 Cor vii 24
(not *unto* which) he was called are the cases of the circumcised and the uncircumcised. They are bidden to seek no change in this respect. Each state in itself is nothing, but not so is "keeping of God's commandments": for the Jew, he means to suggest, circumcision had been included under God's commandments, and this and only this had been binding, while the principle of obedience to God's commandments lay equally on all.

St Paul's dealing with 'meats offered to idols' 1 Cor viii
has already come before us.

In a later chapter we have a striking description of his own policy, if one may so call it. "Being free, he says, I brought myself under bondage by all occasions 1 Cor ix 19
to all men" (*ἐκ πάντων...ἐδούλωσα* not *ἐλεύθερος ἐκ* as commonly taken).

On the other hand the wonderful close of the fifteenth chapter contains one startling phrase, "the 1 Cor xv 56
power of sin is the law," which we could hardly interpret without the aid of the Anti-Judaic arguments in Rom. iv., v., vii., and which shews how deeply St Paul felt the stress of the great controversy.

Judaizing traducers in the Second Epistle

When we enter the second Epistle we find the position changed. The enquiry into the relations between the two Epistles bristles with difficult questions of history and of interpretation of language which we must simply leave on one side. What is at once pertinent to our subject and perfectly clear is the presence of a leaven in the Corinthian Church which is at least connected with Palestinian Judaizing. Its most prominent characteristic is rather personal than doctrinal, and so far reminds us of what we found in the Epistles to the Thessalonians. We have nothing of circumcision, nothing expressly of the law; but we have St Paul repeatedly vindicating his authority and his conduct against traducers who evidently are not representatives of a libertine party, and who must have set up against him the authority of the Palestinian apostles, the

2 Cor xi 5; xii 11 ὑπερλίαν ἀπόστολοι, as he twice calls them[1], who had held converse with the Lord before His Death and Ascension.

The spirit and the letter 2 Cor iii

In one chapter the principle itself for which he was contending comes to the surface for many verses together, in the references to the new covenant of the spirit and the covenant of the letter, the ministration of righteousness with its abiding glory and the ministration of death with its transitory glory on the face of Moses, the unveiling in the spirit and the veil resting on the hearts of the hearers of Moses. And there are other passages where the same tone is more or less distinctly heard. But while the Epistle glows with an intenser heat of fervid life than any other in the New Testament, unless it be the first Epistle of St John, the heat is not that of con-

[1] Compare xi. 22, apparently on the claims of the traducers themselves as Hebrews and Israelites and a seed of Abraham.

troversy. We should hardly know what these flashes of the Pauline Gospel meant if they were not interpreted for us by other Epistles.

The Epistle to the Galatians

Date not important

In the Epistle to the Galatians the question at issue comes to the front vividly and nakedly. I speak of Galatians here partly because this is the most convenient place, partly because Lightfoot has given good reasons—though not all equally good reasons—for fixing Galatians after the second, rather than before the first Epistle to the Corinthians, the order most commonly adopted, especially on the Continent. But this is a point more interesting than important. It is undoubtedly true that we have no right to *assume* the Judaistic controversy to have proceeded *pari passu* in Asia Minor and in European Greece. On the other hand if the circumstances which gave rise to the Epistle to the Galatians had taken place before the second Epistle to the Corinthians was written, we might have expected them to colour St Paul's language about the Corinthian Judaizers.

The question of circumcision for Gentiles

As we all know, this Epistle was written in consequence of a retrogression among the Galatians due to the seductions of Judaizing missionaries, who not only attacked the apostolic authority of St Paul as invalid beside that of the Jerusalem apostles, as men of the same spirit had done at Corinth, but were preaching, and apparently successfully preaching, to the Galatians the necessity of circumcision. Concession to this demand St Paul denounces as virtual apostasy from Gal v 2 f. the Gospel. "Behold I Paul say to you that if ye receive circumcision, Christ will profit you nothing. Yea, I protest again to every man that receiveth circumcision, that he is a debtor to do the whole law."

This is the negative side of the exhortation: but its force rests on the positive side. St Paul was no heated partisan, intolerant of a lesser good through ill-regulated zeal for a greater. No one who in the least understands either his Epistles or the Acts could for a moment conceive St Paul using this language to born Jews. The question at issue was whether heathens, having become Christians, were to be required to become Jews likewise, and that as a matter of essential principle. To concede this was to make void the grace of God and the faith of man: it was to take all the meaning out of such words as Gal iv 6 f. these, "Because ye are sons, God sent forth the Spirit of His Son into our hearts, crying Abba Father. So that thou art no longer a bondservant, but a son: and if a son, then an heir through God."

The Epistle to the Romans

The second Epistle to the Corinthians and the Epistle to the Galatians were apparently written on the way from Ephesus through Macedonia round to

Achaia and Corinth. At length St Paul reached Greece and spent there three months, and then prepared to carry out the intention formed at Ephesus of proceeding to Jerusalem, hoping if all went well to return then to the West and make his way to Rome. But before he sailed, the discovery of a plot of the Jews compelled him to change his course, and again traverse Macedonia. Before sailing, he wrote the Epistle to the Romans.

Ac xx 3

Ac xix 21

Ac xx 3

The contents of the Epistle

Last term[1] I lectured on some of the principal historical questions suggested by that great Epistle. It must be enough now to say that it sums up the Judaistic controversy in a calm and deliberate manner, not for the confutation of present false teachers, but for the stablishment and forewarning of trusted, but only partially instructed, Christians not of the writer's own converting, with a view to the probable future arrival of false teachers among them. It includes the topics of the Epistle to the Galatians, but treats them as parts of a larger whole, and lifts them to a higher level. It exhibits Jew and Gentile as alike condemned by their own shortcomings, and alike saved by the free mercy of God in Christ. The union of both in God's new universal people is the ideal which it presupposes. With this union is associated in St Paul's mind his own contemplated journey to Jerusalem to carry the offering of the Gentile Churches to their Jewish brethren. He is

[1] These lectures are now (1894) in the press.

fully conscious of the dangers that await him there from the hatred of the Jews, and this consciousness gives special solemnity to his mission. But if the offering is accepted and if his life is preserved, he hopes to

Ro xv 32

arrive at Rome the representative of a united Church, and thus with the best of omens to carry his Gospel in person to the centre of the whole civilised world. And meanwhile his apostleship to the Gentiles, to which his main efforts are subservient, has done nothing to make him abhor the unbelieving Jews, whom he knows to be plotting his death, and of whom he might now with ampler experience use the old language of the first Epistle to the Thessalonians. His present language carries on the Lord's own prayer

Lk xxiii 34

on the Cross, "Father, forgive them, for they know not what they do." For their sakes he could wish

Ro ix 3

to be himself anathema from Him who was his Messiah and theirs. Though their unbelief and consequent alienation from God grows more invete-

Ro xi 29

rate day by day, he believes firmly that the gifts and the calling of God are without repentance, and has faith that the distant future will vindicate the unsearchable resources of God's wisdom and mercy.

Close of the Term's Lectures

At this point we must leave both St Paul and the great issue which we have been throughout considering. The subject has proved far too large for the time allotted to it, if it was to be examined in any fruitful detail. We have had to leave untouched not only the whole of post-apostolic Judaistic Christianity, but the records of the latter part of the apostolic age, nay, even St Paul's own later writings and later years. But we can now see that the crisis of Apostolic Christianity was virtually over when St Paul wrote that letter from Corinth or Cenchreæ to Rome, and started for his perilous mission to Jerusalem. At every stage he had vindicated the universality of the new faith and the new covenant; and at every stage he had been implicitly teaching the Gentiles the fulfilment of the Law and the Prophets. In one sense the things of old time had simply passed away: in another sense they had passed away only by becoming new.

LECTURE VI

St Paul at Jerusalem and the Epistles of the Roman Captivity

From Corinth to Jerusalem

No clear trace of Judaizers THE narrative which occupies the last nine chapters of the Acts, comprising St Paul's journey from Corinth to Jerusalem, his imprisonment, and his transportation to Rome, contains but little matter bearing directly on the history of Judaistic Christianity. At two points alone does it manifestly meet us: on the arrival at Jerusalem, and on the arrival at Rome. It is indeed probable enough that the "grievous wolves" of whom St Paul spoke at Miletus to the Ephesian elders as destined after his departure
Ac xx 29 to enter in "not sparing the flock" (perhaps in allusion to our Lord's words about false prophets
Mt vii 15 in sheep's clothing) were chiefly or even wholly Judaizing emissaries. But St Luke gives us no indication to this effect. They are clearly different from the men of the Ephesian Church itself, spoken

of in the next verse; who should speak perverse things to draw away the disciples after themselves.

On the other hand, throughout that part of the narrative which precedes the final embarcation for Italy, we are continually coming across signs of the bitter hostility of the unbelieving Jews to St Paul and his work. A plot of theirs diverts him from his intended course at the outset, intimations of impending danger from their malice are given at Miletus and at Cæsarea, and then come the actual perils of Jerusalem. While this persecution of St Paul by unbelieving Judaism has to be steadily distinguished from the invasion of the Pauline Gospel by the doctrines and practices of Judaistic Christianity, it is morally certain, as we shall see immediately, that the one must have exercised a strong practical influence over the other.

Bitter hostility of the Jews

Ac xx 3

Ac xx 23

Ac xxi 11

Reception at Jerusalem

On the arrival of St Paul and his company at Jerusalem, they were joyfully (ἀσμένως), not grudgingly, welcomed by "the brethren". When we read what follows, we cannot but pause at the apparent vagueness of the phrase "the brethren". It evidently can mean nothing like the whole body of Christians at Jerusalem, and it could not with any propriety be applied to a mere single set of Pauline Christians. Apparently it means those who had the best right, of

Welcomed by 'the Brethren'

Ac xxi 17

one kind or another, to be regarded as legitimate representatives of the whole body. If the Apostles were in Jerusalem, they (or some of them) would naturally be included, but nothing whatever is said of the Apostles or any one of them in the narrative of these eventful days at Jerusalem. On the other hand

after cautious entry

the language used suggests that the city was entered with much precaution and avoidance of observation.

Ac xxi 16 What is said of Mnason, the early disciple from Cyprus, as the destined host of St Paul's company, and his being brought up expressly from Cæsarea to lodge them, implies that it was not thought advisable for St Paul to go to his usual quarters. The next day,

Ac xxi 18 we read, he went in with his travelling companions (σὺν ἡμῖν) to James; and all the elders were present.

The officers of the Church

Whether the other Apostles were in Jerusalem or not, he would naturally put himself in the frankest and most direct relations with St James, who (whether we call him 'bishop' or not—the name is of little consequence) was evidently at the head of the local Church, the Church of Jerusalem.

Similarly the elders are doubtless the *zekênim* or elders who were the officers of the community of Christian Jews at Jerusalem like the *zekênim* of the original Jewish community of Jerusalem. They have been previously mentioned in connexion with two

Ac xi 30 events. They stand alone, quite naturally, as the recipients of the contribution sent by the Church of Antioch for the relief of their famishing brethren in

Judaea. Again, they have a definite place and responsibility by the side of the Apostles in the great conference on the question of the circumcision of Gentile converts. Ac xv 6 etc.

To this, the whole staff of officers of the local Church, St Paul speaks. He greets them, and then describes his successful missionary labours, doubtless those of the last four years. When they had heard the tale, they glorified God. As far as we can tell, they had nothing to blame in the course taken by St Paul; for them the question of the circumcision of Gentiles had ceased, and become a thing of the past. But at the same time they warned him that their own friendliness was not shared by the bulk of the local Church. There were multitudes of Christian Jews living mixed among the general body of Jews, and they had all been led into a state of profound distrust, to say the least, against St Paul, by the assiduous talking and lecturing (κατηχήθησαν) of others to the effect that St Paul had been striving to make all Jews of the Dispersion apostates from the Law, urging them not to circumcise their children or follow the traditional Jewish customs. The statement is shown by all our evidence to have been wholly false, a transference to Jewish converts in the Dispersion, of what was true only in respect of Gentile converts.

Ac xxi 19 f.

Warnings of prejudice

Ac xxi 20 ff.

The speakers who dinned this calumny into the ears of the Jewish Christians of Jerusalem were

arising from Jewish calumny

of course their unbelieving neighbours, who hated St Paul for doing *anything* to open the fold of God to heathens (κωλυόντων ἡμᾶς τοῖς ἔθνεσιν λαλῆ-
1 Thes ii 16 σαι ἵνα σωθῶσιν). How easily they would obtain what they could put forward plausibly as authentic confirmation of the statement, we may see a few verses on, when the Jews from Asia recognised St
Ac xxi 28 f. Paul, and stirred up a tumult against him by declaring that he had brought Greeks into the Temple: on the ground, as St Luke explains, that they had recognised Trophimus the Ephesian as accompanying him in the city. The misrepresentation that St Paul had brought him into the Temple, is exactly analogous to the misrepresentation of St Paul's policy towards Gentile converts, as though he followed it towards Jewish converts likewise.

St Paul in the Temple

The officers' suggestion

To mollify the enmity of the unbelieving Jews was evidently out of the question. But James and the elders might well think it worth while for St Paul to set himself right, if possible, with the multitude of Christian Jews. To have them estranged in feeling either from the great apostle himself, or from the growing Gentile Churches, would be a grievous calamity for the Church as a whole. In such a matter a single significant act would have tenfold greater weight than any number of words; and so

James and the elders suggested that St Paul should join with four Jewish Christians of Jerusalem in the solemn public rites performed in execution of a vow in the Temple, furnishing them with the means of providing the necessary sacrifices, as we know from other sources to have been often done. However little we may know of the details of the proceeding thus suggested, it would clearly contain two important elements: St Paul would be seen performing a Jewish act of religion in the Temple, and he would be seen doing it in company with known Jewish Christians, placing himself on the same level with them, and evidently contributing to their expenses. Ac xxi 23 f.

St Paul's share in the rites

It is an interesting but a difficult question what part he took himself in this matter, beyond accompanying the four votaries and supplying their sacrifices. The words *ἁγνίσθητι σὺν αὐτοῖς*, *ἁγνισθείς*, and *ἡγνισμένον*, are hard to explain if St Paul took no part in the sacred rites on his own account. Yet the time spoken of appears too short for him to begin and complete a vow in. It is therefore more probable, though not mentioned in Acts, that he was already proposing to offer sacrifice in the Temple on his own account, possibly in connexion with a previous vow, possibly also, I cannot but suspect, in connexion with the Gentile contribution to the Jewish Christians, not mentioned in c. xxi., but clearly mentioned in xxiv. 17 (*ἐλεημοσύνας ποιήσων εἰς τὸ ἔθνος μου*) as well as in his own Epistles. The Ac xxi 24, 26; xxiv 18 contribution was probably presented at the meeting with James, and then and there gratefully accepted. On such an occasion it may well be that St Paul proposed to celebrate this happy event by a solemn peace-offering in the Temple. This would account

Ac xxiv 17 for the καὶ προσφοράς (hardly to be explained by the four votaries' offerings alone); and it gives

Ro xv 16 additional point to what is said of ἡ προσφορὰ τῶν ἐθνῶν in the Epistle to the Romans.

Effect on local Church unknown

Howsoever this may be, St Paul at once acted on the advice of St James; with what results towards the discontented part of the Christian community at Jerusalem we know not, for the attack made upon him by Jews before the close of the acts of purification is the subject of St Luke's next section, and we hear no more of St James or his Church in the Acts.

St Paul's consistency

The act here ascribed to St Paul is the subject of much doubt to many critics. They cannot believe that the uncompromising Apostle of the Gentiles could behave so like a mere Jew. I do not know however of any evidence that makes it in the least improbable: on the contrary it throws a clear light on St Paul's own position, and thus on the true nature of the differences between Judaistic Christianity proper and the transitional states liable to be confounded with it, which were a necessity of the Apostolic age. We shall look in vain in St Paul's words or acts for any sign that he took advantage for himself of the kind of liberty which he so passionately claimed for Gentile Christians. Little as we know about the vows in which he on this occasion made himself a participator, it so happens that we have already learned casually of a similar vow taken upon him independently, characterised in the same way by the shaving of the head which took place at Cenchreæ. This precedent shews how little likely it is that he would be merely acting a part, in adopting the advice given him at Jerusalem. cf. Mt xvii 27 Ac xviii 18

Before the Sanhedrin

Similarly, when he stood before the high priests and Sanhedrin, however little we may know how he failed to recognise the High Priest Hananiah, he was but true to his own principles when he acknowledged him as the ruler of his people, of whom, by Divine command, he was not to speak evil. What followed was more open to misunderstanding, his proclaiming himself to be a "Pharisee, a son of Pharisees". But here too he gave truthful utterance to his own purposes and convictions. From Pharisaism, in so far as it meant zeal for the highest objects of Jewish faith, he had never departed and never could depart, though he had learned to cherish fresh objects of faith. His quarrel with Pharisaism was on the means which it upheld and adopted for carrying out the high ends which it professed to value; on its principles of action, not on its consecrated watchwords. His opening words indeed contain a claim which Ac xxiii 5 Ac xxiii 6 Ac xxvi 5 ff.; 22 f.

includes all the rest: it is not a virtuous life but a loyally Jewish life that he professes to have lived when he says "with all good conscience πεπολίτευμαι τῷ θεῷ till this day", the reference being to the Jewish πολίτευμα, the commonwealth of God.

Ac xxiii 1

St Paul at Rome

Attitude of Jews in Rome

We now pass to the last chapter of the Acts, and St Paul's interview with the leading men of the Jews at Rome. To them he uses language much like the language which he had used at Jerusalem. He addresses them as brethren, declaring that he had "done nothing contrary to the people or to the customs of the fathers," and that it was "for the sake of the hope of Israel that he had to wear those chains." They on their part state that they knew the Christian αἵρεσις to be everywhere spoken against; but they had received neither letters nor envoys from Jerusalem about Paul himself. Hence it is clear that the emissaries sent from the Pharisaic party to stir up opposition to St Paul in Asia Minor and Greece had not gone as far as Rome. Possibly his long imprisonment had seemed to make such a step unnecessary.

Ac xxviii 17 ff.

Ac xxviii 21 f.

Apparently no Judaizers

Respecting the existence or non-existence of an anti-Pauline Jewish party among the Christians of Rome we learn nothing directly. It is however most unlikely that any such movement could have arisen at Rome without the knowledge of the leading Jews of Rome; and no difference among the brethren who greeted St Paul on his arrival is in any way indicated by St Luke: nay, there is not improbably a pregnant significance in his words that when St Paul saw them come to meet him at Appii Forum and the Three Taverns, he thanked God and took courage, as though he had feared the possibility of an unfriendly or at least divided reception. Ac xxviii 15

Three years had passed since the Epistle to the Romans was written. At that time he had apparently no information of the existence of a Judaizing party among Roman Christians, though one of the postscripts to the Epistle, written in peculiarly guarded and reticent language, seems intended as a warning with a view to the probable contingency of the arrival of such disturbers of their peace. But, as far as we can see, the foreboding had not been fulfilled. Ro xvi 17–20

The good results of St Paul's imprisonment

In this too we may once more reasonably trace the operation of St Paul's imprisonment. It was not unnatural for Jews and Judaizers to suppose that, now that he was shut up safe at Cæsarea, the Pauline movement in the West would languish for want of the impetus given by his personal force, and might safely be left to itself: nor were the circumstances of his transportation Romewards likely to give rise to apprehensions of future triumphs at Rome. These are in truth but instances of what we may well suspect to be widely extended results of that imprisonment. In the eyes of men, probably of Christians themselves, it might well seem that the progress of the Gospel had received a dangerous check when the Apostle was thus violently snatched away from his ever advancing labours. But the Providence of God ruled it otherwise. Not only was St Paul himself thus rescued from imminent perils of death and reserved for fresh work in a fresh sphere, but his disappearance can hardly have failed to cause some slackening of the fierce antagonisms which had arisen, and thus to give the newly founded Churches better opportunities for quiet growth. Such a state of things had dangers of its own, and it afforded no real security against Judaistic or other doctrinal propaganda: but it may well have been a necessary stage in the infancy of the Gentile Churches.

The Epistle to the Philippians

Judaizers in Philippi

If however the Judaistic propaganda became, at least for a time, less active, the Epistle to the Philippians, the first Epistle of St Paul's captivity, shews how much reason St Paul still had to fear its operations in Macedonia. When the Epistle is apparently drawing to its close with the same almost unbroken serenity which rests on it from the beginning, it suddenly launches forth into a vehement warning against those who falsely prided themselves on their circumcision and high Jewish privileges, in

Phil iii 1

which the Apostle might himself have boasted had he not set himself to pursue an altogether different ideal. The last portion of this passage, which I feel sure has the same false teaching in view, not that of an antinomian tendency, uses even stronger language, calling the Judaizers the enemies of the cross of Christ, contrasting the earthly elements of external observance involved in the visible πολίτευμα, to which they clung, with the true invisible Christian πολίτευμα in the heavens.

Phil iii 17ff. cf. Gal vi 12, 14

The later Epistles of the First Captivity

When we pass on to the remaining group of three Epistles belonging to the first Roman captivity, we encounter what is apparently a new or at least a different phase of Judaistic Christianity.

The short private letter to Philemon naturally is silent about it.

The 'Ephesians' free from controversy

The general Epistle which from its primary address we call the Epistle to the Ephesians is equally silent about it, though for a different reason. Its purpose is wholly positive. It may well be that some of the Churches addressed were free from the evil leaven: but at all events, for one and all it was important to have this exposition of the heights and depths of the Gospel set before them undisturbed by any vein of controversial writing.

We see from the first Epistle to the Corinthians

that St Paul was at a much earlier time anxious lest the Gospel should be thought to consist exclusively of those simpler elements of it to which he deliberately confined himself in the teaching of Churches still in their infancy; and that he was likely, if opportunity offered, in due time to give utterance to those other
1 Cor iii 2 elements of it which he called 'strong meat' as distinguished from that 'milk for babes'. The Asiatic Churches had now apparently reached a stage when in carrying out this wish, he would be best providing for their practical needs at the time. This applies to both 'Ephesians' and Colossians. But in the Epistle to the Colossians the positive teaching is intermingled with definitely controversial warnings. Even these warnings however leave room for much uncertainty, both as to the precise nature of the false teaching, and as to its origin; and it is important to distinguish between distinct evidence and more or less conjectural inferences.

The Colossian Heresy.

The crucial passages Col ii 8; 16-23

The definite warnings are contained in two passages, ii. 8 and ii. 16—23, ii. 16 being in reality a resumption of ii. 8 after the positive exposition into which ii. 8 passes. In other words, the one verse ii. 8 is a somewhat general description of the danger spoken of afterwards in detail. It will be best to begin with this more detailed second passage.

The opening words Μὴ οὖν τις ὑμᾶς κρινέτω

suggest the presence of teachers who were striving to impose on the Colossians certain precepts as matters of conscience. They are the subject first (*vv.* 16—19) of direct admonition, then (*vv.* 20—23) of expostulation and argument. *The danger present*

We have, to begin with, two forms of observance, the observance of a difference of foods, "in meat and (or "or") in drink," and again the observance of sacred seasons "in the matter of a feast or new moon or sabbath." The first of these, the difference of foods, might, as we shall see, or might not, be Jewish: the second can be only Jewish (*σαββάτων* being decisive): while all three words together are a Jewish phrase. The added comment that these things are a shadow of the things to come, the true body corresponding to them being found only in the Christ (almost the language of the Epistle to the Hebrews), is equally decisive; and the form of the sentence shews that the comment covers all five heads. It is urged on the other hand that though *βρώσει* might have a Jewish reference, *πόσει* could not: to which it is a sufficient answer to point to Heb. ix 1 (*ἐπὶ βρώμασιν καὶ πόμασιν*), where, account being taken of the Rabbinical developments and extensions of the Levitical precepts, the Jewish reference is undeniable. *Signs of Jewish influence* Heb x 1 Heb ix 1

In the next verse we have a quite fresh point. Whatever be the meaning of *θέλων ἐν ταπεινοφροσύνῃ*, the phrase *θρησκείᾳ τῶν ἀγγέλων* is sufficiently *Angel Worship* Col ii 18 distinct. Worship of angels must have been one characteristic of the false teaching; and though it is not directly referred to elsewhere in the Epistle, its indirect influence may be traced in the various passages which set forth the Son of God as holding the supreme place in the economy of creation and history, far above all invisible, as well as visible created beings.

The elements of the world

In the following verses we have more than one sign that we are still on Jewish ground. The "ele-
Col ii 20 ments of the world" of *v.* 20 can hardly be other
Gal iv 3, 9 cf. 10 than the Jewish "elements" of the Epistle to the Galatians: and the precepts of abstinence referred
Col ii 21 f. to in *v.* 21 are said to be "*according to the commands and teachings* of men", a phrase borrowed from
Mt xv 9 Mk vii 7 Is. xxix. 13, and applied by the Lord Himself to the Pharisees.

Col ii 23 The very difficult next verse need not delay us, as its points come chiefly from *vv.* 16, 18.

The tradition of men

Going back to the general terms used in *v.* 8, we find as in *v.* 20 "the elements of the world", and also, "the tradition of men", a phrase evidently answering to "the teachings and commands of men,"
Mk vii 8 and similarly used of the Pharisees in the Gospel in close juxtaposition with the quotation from Isaiah. The phrase is the more remarkable because this is the only place where St Paul speaks disparagingly of "tradition" or "traditions".

'Philosophy and vain deceit'

But we likewise find these two phrases combined

with the apparently very different phrase τῆς φιλο-σοφίας καὶ κενῆς ἀπάτης. There cannot be a doubt of the identity of the subject matter throughout: i.e. the supposition that St Paul is dealing with the teaching of two independent sets of men, the one philosophic and the other Judaic, is absolutely untenable[1]. But the phrase itself is extremely difficult. Col ii 8

The force of the article

What is the force of the article before φιλο-σοφίας? It is certainly not otiose: the words do not mean what they would have meant with *no* article, i.e. simply 'philosophy'.

If again the τῆς were meant to couple φιλοσοφίας and κενῆς ἀπάτης together, the meaning would be 'that which is at once philosophy and vain deceit,' which gives no real sense here. The coupling could not be meant to express "*that* philosophy (as distinguished from more solid philosophy) which is vain deceit".

It only remains to take τῆς with φιλοσοφίας alone, as having the normal individualising force of the article, "*that* philosophy," which we may fill up either as "that philosophy of his" or "that philosophy which you know of" or best as both together "that philosophy of his which you know of[2]".

[1] Cf. Lightfoot's *Colossians*, pp. 74 ff.

[2] Somewhat similar is 1 Cor i 21 ἐπειδὴ γὰρ ἐν τῇ σοφίᾳ τοῦ θεοῦ οὐκ ἔγνω ὁ κόσμος διὰ τῆς σοφίας τὸν θεόν (preceded however by οὐχὶ ἐμώρανεν ὁ θεὸς τὴν σοφίαν τοῦ κόσμου), where the simple article doubtless hints that the wisdom spoken of was not only the wisdom of the world of old but also similar in character to the wisdom affected by the Corinthians. Cf. von Soden *Jahrb. f. Prot. Th.* 1885 p. 366.

This Philosophy Ethical not Theosophic

But then what was the nature of this particular φιλοσοφία? The form of the sentence seems to me to shew that it was not merely taught by the same men who taught subservience to human tradition and the rudiments of the world, but that its own subject matter was this very subservience. If so, the common assumption that some sort of theosophic speculation is intended falls to the ground.

The name assumed to mask its Jewish character

Such phrases as ἡ Ἰουδαικὴ φιλοσοφία in Philo prove nothing, the distinctive force of the phrase lying in the adjective or other qualifying words, and φιλοσοφία being used with the utmost generality for the sake of Hellenic readers, whereas in the Epistle to the Colossians τῆς φιλοσοφίας is itself the distinctive term. It seems probable therefore that the particular movement in favour of these particular Jewish observances at Colossæ laid claim by the mouth of its leaders to be preeminently founded on philosophy; they may even have called it "the philosophy". This would be merely a fresh example of a widely spread tendency of that age to disarm Western prejudice against things Jewish by giving them a quasi-Hellenic varnish.

Esoteric

Moreover, 'angel-worship' might easily be treated as an esoteric lore, and distinctions of foods and days as the perfection of a refined morality above the level of the common multitude. This latter representation would indeed find a kind of foundation in the increasing stress laid on ethics as distinguished from other branches of philosophy in those late days, and that in the Greek-speaking East hardly less than among the Romans.

Moreover, this disposition to treat ethics as the true substantial philosophy was often[1] accompanied by a further disposition to lay special stress on the negative and as it were abstinential side of ethics (to which the Colossian distinctions belong). At a later time φιλοσοφία and the cognate words are found used almost technically for the anchorite life and principles. I do not know of a distinct instance before the Apologia Origenis of Pamphilus (p. 298 Lomm.); but the usage is very common in Eusebius and in later Greek Fathers. This late usage, if not descended from an earlier mode of speech exemplified in the Colossian φιλοσοφία, is at least illustrative of it. *Ascetic*

The addition of κενὴ ἀπάτη was a natural way of indicating that there was a real speciousness in the claim set up for this φιλοσοφία, this professed love of wisdom. It is interesting to observe that in the cognate Epistle to the Ephesians similar language is used (μηδεὶς ὑμᾶς ἀπατάτω κενοῖς λόγοις) in reference to the opposite exhibition of a licentious antinomianism as a high kind of wisdom. *Specious attractiveness* Eph v 6 cf iv 22

In interpreting τῆς φιλοσοφίας not as a speculative

[1] Illustrations on Jewish ground occur in the Greek Jewish tract, or homily, beginning φιλοσοφώτατον λόγον ἐπιδείκνυσθαι μέλλων, called 4 Maccabees, see especially i. 1—9; v. 6—23; vii. 7—9; and in Philo *Cong. erud. grat.* 14 (M. i. 530 sub fin.); *Opif. mun.* 43 (M. i. 30); *de Septen.* 6 (M. ii. 282).

theosophy lying outside of Jewish usages but as embodying the plea put forward on their behalf, we are further supported by the fact that *σοφία* is the word chosen further on, in *v.* 23, (*ἅτινά ἐστιν* Col ii 23 *λόγον μὲν ἔχοντα σοφίας*) to express the nature of the plausibility of the usages in question.

New elements

Apart from this phrase there is no indication that the Colossian Judaism included a philosophy, in the sense of a speculative doctrine. The worship of angels was assuredly a widely spread Jewish habit of mind at this time: the Epistle to the Hebrews shews Heb i, ii how prevalent it was where there is no sign of what we should call a philosophy. At the same time it is true that this Colossian Judaism is not identical with what we have encountered in earlier epistles. Not only is the angel-worship a new element, but the principle of the whole is to a great extent changed. The question of the permanent bindingness of the Law on all men admitted to covenant with God passes out of sight, and with it the question as to the necessity of circumcision. Circumcision is indeed prominent in the remarkable doctrinal passage ii. Col ii 11–15 11—15, where the nailing to the Cross is represented as itself, so to speak, a complete and final circumcision; and this suggests that at Colossæ the Mosaic rite of circumcision was still invested with a dignity which no longer rightly belonged to it. Again, in the singular language of iii. 5, which describes vices as "the members upon the earth" which are to be done to death, a latent reference to circumcision may be traced with fair probability. But in both passages the language used is hardly such as would be used of what was then and there a burning question of practice. Col iii 5

The questions directly dealt with are not such matters as the function of the Law, and the relation of the Old Covenant to the New, but practical questions, questions of difference of foods and difference of days and angel-worship, dealt with to a great extent on universal grounds. At the outset indeed the ceremonial distinctions do not appear to be condemned in themselves: the Colossians are simply warned in a strain hardly different from that of Rom. xiv. not to allow any one to "judge" them in such. But the next section implies that the Colossians were actually carried away by the spirit in which these observances were advocated, and indeed rebukes them for it. Col ii 20–23

The Colossian 'Humility'

In the whole passage it would be too much to say that the old arguments from the transitory nature of the Law are entirely absent: they survive in the language about "the shadow of the things to come", and about "dying with Christ from the elements of the world": but at least equal stress is laid on grounds of general religious morality, and on the practical inconsistency of the Colossian ways with full recognition of the Lord's person and work.

It is probably in this sense that we must understand the enigmatical ταπεινοφροσύνη of ii. 18 and 23, which seems to mean a grovelling habit of mind, choosing lower things as the primary sphere of re-
Col iii 1 ligion, and not τὰ ἄνω, the region in which Christ is seated at God's right hand.

Its relation to the doctrine of the Person of Christ

A question may be raised whether St Paul meant by this word to impute to the Colossians only (1) a habit of mind which made it difficult for them to see what was involved in the full belief concerning Christ's nature as really held by them, or (2) a defectiveness in the belief itself. The language of the controversial passage ii. 6—iii. 4 would be sufficiently explained by the former supposition, an explanation favoured by its opening sentence, and especially by the choice of such a word as περιπατεῖτε. On the other hand the connexion in which the warning of ii. 4 stands (τοῦτο λέγω ἵνα μηδεὶς ὑμᾶς παραλογίζηται ἐν πιθανολογίᾳ following upon Χριστοῦ, ἐν ᾧ εἰσιν πάντες οἱ θησαυροί) implies that St Paul's chief fear was of doctrinal error respecting Christ Himself. The truth probably is that St Paul had no evidence that the Colossians had actually given up the belief in which they had been
cf Col i 6 originally instructed, but that he did fear their falling back from it under alien influences, when they ought to have been rather advancing in the knowledge and application of it. Thus ii. 7 (βεβαιού-

μενοι τῇ πίστει καθὼς ἐδιδάχθητε) obtains full force: see also i. 23 (μὴ μετακινούμενοι ἀπὸ τῆς ἐλπίδος τοῦ εὐαγγελίου οὗ ἠκούσατε). The alien influence thus dreaded is such as might naturally be found in any form of Judaistic Christianity. To accept Jesus as the Christ without any adequate enlargement of current Jewish conceptions as to what was included in Messiahship could hardly fail to involve either a limitation of His nature to the human sphere, or at most a counting of Him among the angels.

Differences from Palestinian Judaism

This is all, I think, that can be ascertained with reasonable probability from the Epistle as to the special form of Judaistic Christianity which was gaining ground among the Colossians. In enquiring about its origin, we are thus dispensed from the need of trying to discover for it any peculiar or extraneous sources. We are apparently on common Jewish ground. The points actually condemned among the Colossians are to be found in the Epistle to the Hebrews, i.e. among the Palestinian Jewish Christians. The differences between the Judaistic Christianity of Colossæ and of Palestine are two, negative and positive. Negatively, as we have seen, Colossæ does not seem to have been troubled about the permanent bindingness of the Law and all that is involved in this, while in Palestine this idea had naturally great force. Positively, at Colossæ the Jewish ways were commended to Christians by the specious names of wisdom and philosophy, of which in this connexion we hear nothing in Palestine. The two differences are not independent but complementary: they consist merely in the substitution of one authority for another. Both differences need no further explanation than the one obvious difference of external position. In Palestine, as also in regions invaded by Palestinian emissaries (e.g. Antioch and Galatia), the Christian belief and practice are affected by the central or Pharisaic Judaism of Jerusalem; in Colossæ they are affected by the Judaism of the Dispersion.

Comparison with the Roman Judaism

This conclusion is confirmed by comparison with Rom. xiv. That chapter (and indirectly xv. 1—13) is apparently called forth by disputes in the Roman Church about differences of foods and differences of days.

Now it is a remarkable fact respecting this Epistle to the Romans, as I have before had occasion to point out, that while it discusses the question of the Law with great emphasis and fulness, it does so without the slightest sign that there is a reference to a controversy then actually existing in the Roman Church. St Paul is most anxious to instruct the Romans carefully on this great question (especially in the earlier part of the Epistle), but it is with reference, as far as we can see, to a possible future invasion of aggressive Judaizers. To such persons there is probably a reference in the short passage xvi. 17—20, but it is only in one of the postscripts to the Epistle, and the language used, with all its vehemence, is most carefully guarded. And again, as we saw the other day, the last chapter of Acts p. 113 attests that even at that later time the Roman Church was unmolested by the emissaries from Jerusalem.

Thus the state of things noticed in c. xiv., if (as seems probable) of Jewish origin, must come from the, so to speak, primitive conditions of the Roman Church, antecedent to any invasion from without: in other words, from the Judaism of the Dispersion out of which at least a large proportion of the original members of the Roman Church must have come. In this chapter not only is there no reference to a burning controversy, but no reference to Judaism in relation to Christianity in any form. The matter is dealt with simply as one of individual conscience, the conscience on the side of the restrictions spoken of being doubtless due to a survival of inherited custom.

The reason for the contrast

But the contrast in tone between the two epistles is most interesting and instructive. To the Romans St Paul pleads for tolerance and gentleness towards "the weak ones", as he calls them, who conscientiously clung to the differences of foods and days. At Colossæ it was no question of retaining customs, but of introducing new practices among people who had originally received a purer faith, such practices moreover being valued for the sake of a false principle, to say nothing of being associated with an angel-worship which dishonoured the Lord Himself.

Supposed connexion with Essenism

There is much and high modern authority for tracing the teaching condemned by St Paul at Colossæ to Essene influences; and in lecturing on the Epistle to the Romans, I spoke of that as the most probable origin. But further examination has convinced me that this is too much to say.

There is no tangible evidence for Essenism out of Palestine. (1) The problem of the tract *De vita contemplativa* attributed to Philo and of the so-called *Therapeutae* described in it, is as yet unsolved. (2) As regards Asia Minor in particular, the two supposed pieces of evidence for Essenism break down completely:—(*a*) Magic, which we find common in this region (as probably in all others), is said to have been practised by the Essenes, but it is nowise a prominent feature of their life, and there is no sign of it at Colossæ:—(*b*) The fourth book of the Sibylline Oracles, apparently written in S. W. Asia Minor, though supposed by some to have been written by a Christian and by others by an ordinary Jew seems (though confident speaking would be misplaced) to belong, as Ewald and others have supposed, to a Hemerobaptist. Now to judge by the very little that we really know of Hemerobaptism, it does offer some analogies to Essenism, but no clear signs of actual affinity can be made out: nor again is there anything to connect it with the Colossian tendencies.

If we knew more of the Judaism of the Dispersion, we might conceivably be able to find some definite form of influence at work, here and also in a lesser degree at Rome: but there is no need to postulate anything more than the concurrence of the most obvious influences.

Possible Greek influences

As regards the pretensions to "wisdom" and "philosophy" it is needless to think of outlying or outlandish sects of philosophy or religion, or anything except the commonest Greek influences which would act upon many members of the Jewish Dispersion in towns of Asia Minor. An excellent illustration is afforded by the Corinthian Church. Among them a pride of wisdom proved, by the side of a pride of eloquence, a special snare, and had party spirit and factiousness for its practical outcome, and this, as we may gather from Col. iii. 12—15, was likewise becoming the case at Colossæ. But with all this glorification of "wisdom" (so called) at Corinth, there is no sign of what is popularly called Gnosticism, though knowledge (γνῶσις) as well as "wisdom" was a catchword there: whether it was a catchword also at Colossæ, we have no means of knowing. The truth is, the claim to be adopting a more highly cultivated form of religion, and the application to it of the common catchwords of Greek eulogy, might easily take many different forms. Whether in this case there was also an accessory influence from some kind of popular Greek ethical philosophy, it is impossible to say: the presence of such an influence is undeniably possible, but there is no need to assume it.

1 Cor viii 1 f, 11; i 5; xiii 2, 8

LECTURE VII

The Pastoral Epistles

The question of genuineness

We come now to the Pastoral Epistles. On the critical question of their genuineness I must say very little. The case of the Pastoral Epistles is by no means like that of other Epistles of St Paul which have been pronounced by critics to come from another hand on grounds which it is difficult to discuss seriously. There are features of the Pastoral Epistles which legitimately provoke suspicion. To the best of my belief, however, they are genuine, and that not merely in parts: the theory of large early interpolations does not work out at all well in detail.

Some groundless objections

While they present some difficulties which still await explanation, there is, I think, no real force in some of the objections which have been most strongly felt. Thus, (1) it is true that the Pastoral Epistles imply a period of activity in St Paul's life of which we have no other evidence: but neither is there any evidence against it, our ignorance being here complete. (2) The ecclesiastical arrangements are said to be the fiction of a later time: but this is mainly owing to misunderstanding of the ecclesiastical arrangements really implied; partly also to arbitrary assumptions as to the date of institutions. (3) The doctrines condemned are said to belong to no earlier time than the Second Century; but this, as we shall see, is due to a misunderstanding of what the doctrines really are.

Real difficulties

The real difficulties lie in the field of language, and of ideas as embodied in language. The differences, however, in this respect from St Paul's other epistles, become much less significant when we notice similar differences between the Epistles of the captivity and those of earlier date. Much of them may be reasonably taken to be due to changed circumstances, and especially to the fact that the recipients were trusted individual disciples and deputies, not miscellaneous churches. The main points connected with this subject have been discussed, and for the most part admirably discussed, by Bernhard Weiss of Berlin in the edition which he substituted last year for Huther's edition of the Pastoral Epistles in the New Testament Commentary begun by Meyer.

Weiss on the teaching condemned in the Epistles

As regards the erroneous teaching condemned in the Pastoral Epistles, which is the only part of the subject which directly concerns us now, Weiss (pp. 17—29) clears the ground by some important distinctions. He points out, (1) that we must distinguish prophecies about future false teachers from warnings about the present. He admits, however, and this has to be remembered, that prophecies of this kind imply that the germs, to say the least, of the future evils are already perceptible. The passages under this head are 1 Tim. iv. 1—3; 2 Tim. iii. 1—5; with its sequel iv. 3 f. (2) The perversities of individuals must not be taken as direct evidence for the general streams of false teaching. So perhaps 1 Tim. i. 20 (Hymenæus and Alexander); certainly 2 Tim. ii. 17 f. (Hymenæus and Philetus). Here again, however, it may well be that the individual aberrations are regarded as extreme cases of the natural outcome of more widely spread tendencies. (3) Non-Christian teachers, the corrupters of Christian belief, must not be confounded with misguided Christians. So probably Titus i. 15 f.

On the other hand, there is no indication, any more than in the Epistle to the Colossians, that there were, so to speak, different schools of error among Christians. The various tendencies spoken of were to all appearance combined in the same persons, and they were members of the Church, though the suggestions to which they lent too ready an ear may have come from without.

Again, just as in the Epistle to the Colossians, several obvious marks of Judaism are present: yet it cannot be a Pharisaic Judaism such as had previously confronted St Paul, there being again no debate about circumcision or the prerogatives of Israel, and St Paul's treatment of the matter being again quite unlike what we find in the Epistles to the Galatians and to the Romans.

No specifically Gnostic terms

On the other hand it was not unnatural that the phrase ψευδώνυμος γνῶσις should lead some Fathers of the latter part of the Second Century to see a reference to the heretics of their own or immediately preceding times who prided themselves on a γνῶσις. Still more natural was it that the same identification should be made in modern times when the term 'Gnostic' had lost its original narrow reference and become inclusive of a wide range of teachers and schools. But there is no other evidence. 1 Tim vi 20

There is not the faintest sign that such words as ἄφθαρτος, αἰών, ἐπιφάνεια have any reference to what we call Gnostic terms. The γενεαλογίαι, whatever they may be, cannot conceivably in this connexion (see especially Tit. iii. 9 where the word is preceded by μωρὰς ζητήσεις and followed by ἔριν καὶ μάχας νομικάς) be long strings of emanations of æons or angels, which must moreover in that case have been expressly indicated.

One phrase in the Epistle to Titus, θεὸν ὁμολογοῦσιν εἰδέναι, spoken of the external seducers of the Christians, is, as Weiss points out, by itself almost sufficient to make the reference impossible: ὁμολογοῦσιν could never have been used of men whose Tit i 16 characteristic it was to profess to have a peculiar and superlative knowledge of God.

Most decisive of all is the fact on which Weiss justly insists, that the duty laid on Timothy and Titus is not that of refuting deadly errors, but of keeping themselves clear, and warning others to keep clear, of barren and mischievous trivialities usurping the office of religion.

The curious word ἑτεροδιδασκαλεῖ in 1 Tim. i. 3; vi. 3 must certainly not be interpreted by the associations adhering to the element ἑτερο- as derived from the later ecclesiastical, not classical, sense of ἑτερόδοξος. It points rather to unfitness and irrelevance of teaching, the sense of ἕτερος being substantially as in the πνεῦμα ἕτερον, εὐαγγέλιον ἕτερον of 2 Cor. xi. 4 and εὐαγγέλιον ἕτερον of Gal. i. 6, with which we may compare the διδαχαῖς ποικίλαις καὶ ξέναις (evidently about Jewish observances) of Heb. xiii. 9.

Essenism at least uncertain

It does not follow that these considerations are equally fatal to the supposition that the influences spoken of at Ephesus and in Crete were connected with a speculative form of Judaism out of which some forms of "Gnosticism" may later have been developed. Cerinthus must clearly be left out of account, for want of tangible points of identity: but it would be rash in our ignorance to assume that no other representatives of Gnosticizing Judaism have existed. As regards Essenism there is again a want of identical characteristics; Weiss, who here is very guarded in his language, points to the growing inclination to attribute the tendencies spoken of in Colossians and Romans xiv. to an Essene origin as the most attractive feature of the supposition that the Pastoral Epistles likewise imply Essene origination.

What were 'the genealogies'?

But it seems to me that there is a total want of evidence for anything pointing to even rudimentary Gnosticism or Essenism. First, as regards the *γενεαλογίαι* referred to just now. The phrase is undoubtedly obscure to us, and cannot well be explained, as Weiss explains it, by 'allegorisings of genealogies'; nor by the bare text of such genealogies; any more than by genealogies of æons, angels, or other invisible beings. What seems to be the true explanation is suggested by the similarity between the combination *μύθοις καὶ γενεαλογίαις ἀπεράντοις* in 1 Tim. i. 4 and the combination *περὶ τὰς γενεαλογίας καὶ μύθους* in Polyb. ix. 2. 1. In the preceding chapter (ix. 1. 4) Polybius, apparently quoting Ephorus, takes credit to himself for his 'austere' (or, as we should say, 'dry') narrative, which refrained from enticing the reader by *ὁ γενεαλογικὸς τρόπος*. This language is rightly explained by his editors to refer to the Greek historians before Ephorus whose histories of early times were full of the mythologies of early legend, and the stories of the births of the demigod founders of states. So Diodorus Siculus iv. 1, referring repeatedly to *τὰς παλαιὰς μυθολογίας*, includes in them *ἡ ποικιλία καὶ τὸ πλῆθος τῶν γενεαλογουμένων ἡρῴων τε καὶ ἡμιθέων* καὶ τῶν ἄλλων ἀνδρῶν. Several of these early historians[1] or 'logographers' are known to have written books of this kind entitled Γενεαλογίαι or Γενεαλογικά. Thus, though the term doubtless in the first instance meant genealogies proper, it came to include all the early tales adherent, as it were, to the births of founders etc. This probably explains how it is that Philo[2] divides the Pentateuch first into history and law (commands and prohibitions); and then subdivides the history into the account of creation and τὸ γενεαλογικόν, of which, he says, part refers to the punishment of the impious, part to the honour of the righteous. That is, he includes under τὸ γενεαλογικόν all the primitive human history in the Pentateuch, without special reference to the contained genealogies; though these[3] helped the analogy with the works of the Greek γενεαλόγοι. He uses the term in no depreciatory sense; but otherwise with apparently the same inclusiveness as ordinary Greek writers. Now if Philo could apply this term to the historical part of the Pentateuch, it would *a fortiori* be applicable to the rank growth of legend respecting the patriarchs and other heroes of early Mosaic history which had grown up among the Jews, both in Hebrew and in Greek, before the time of the

[1] So Hecataeus (Müller *Fragm. Hist. Græc.* i. 25—30), Acusilaus (*ibid.* 100—103), Simonides the younger (*ibid.* ii. 42), who bore the title ὁ Γενεαλόγος, as did also Pherecydes. Cf. Josephus *Ap.* i. 3.

[2] *De Vita Moys.* ii. 8 [ii. 141].

[3] Cf. Gen. ii. 4, v. 1, x. 1, xxxviii. 2.

Apostles. Technically, this legendary matter would be included in the Haggada, or illustrative element of commentary on the Old Testament, one branch of which was of a historical or legendary character[1]. So far as it is extant still, it is to be found comparatively little in the Talmud, much more in the Midrash, partly also in Philo and Josephus. But we can perhaps form a still better conception of it from the book of Jubilees (extant only in translations), the legends of which are strung upon a basis of numbered generations. Interesting as matter of this kind is for us as a religious and literary phenomenon, it might with good reason be condemned by St Paul as trashy and unwholesome stuff, when he found it creeping from the Jewish into the Christian communities of Asia Minor and Crete, and occupying men's minds to the exclusion of solid and lifegiving nutriment.

'Questioning' ethical not speculative

In 1 Tim. i. 4 the *γενεαλογίαι* are said to afford matter for *ἐκζητήσεις* rather than for Divine stewardship exercised in faith, the wise apportionment of religious truth, and in the list in Tit. iii. 9 they are preceded by *μωρὰς ζητήσεις*: these words might no doubt mean speculations such as e.g. we associate with Gnosticism: but they may just as well mean simply the exercise of idle curiosity. In 1 Tim. i. 7 it is apparently implied that the persons spoken of aspired to be *νομοδιδάσκαλοι*: in Titus the *γενεαλογίαι* are followed by *ἔριν καὶ μάχας νομικάς*, all alike being

[1] See Schürer, § 25, 2, pp. 278—283 Germ. II. i. 339—350 Eng.

pronounced to be unprofitable and vain as opposed to things *καλὰ καὶ ὠφέλιμα*. Here then we seem to have a reference to the trivial casuistry which constituted no small part of the Halacha, the other great province of Jewish teaching, the province of precept and external observance. Thus all hangs together if *γενεαλογίαι* has here the meaning suggested by the language of Polybius and Philo.

'Profane babblings'

Another phrase has with still greater plausibility been supposed to refer to Gnosticism, *τὰς βεβήλους κενοφωνίας καὶ ἀντιθέσεις τῆς ψευδωνύμου γνώσεως*, against which St Paul warns Timothy at the end of his first Epistle.

The single adjective *βέβηλος* has occurred already in iv. 7 in conjunction with the *μῦθοι* (*τοὺς δὲ βεβήλους καὶ γραώδεις μύθους παραιτοῦ*): it expresses not so much profanity in the modern sense as the absence of any Divine or sacred character.

The full phrase *τὰς βεβήλους κενοφωνίας* recurs in 2 Tim. ii. 16, where the evil fruits of such speech are evidently distinguished from its own less heinous evil: out of it proceeds a downward progress to a lower level of *ἀσέβεια*, no longer merely the absence of a religious spirit, but positive impiety: and of this ultimate result the error of Hymenæus and Philetus respecting the Resurrection is given as an example in the matter of faith.

'Oppositions' not Marcionite

Then come the *ἀντιθέσεις τῆς ψευδωνύμου γνώσεως*. It was not unnatural to think of Marcion's book of

'Ἀντιθέσεις, 'Oppositions' of the Old and New Testaments. But the reference is really inconceivable. Such a work with such a purpose would never have been designated by the author of the Epistle by a mere word like this as part of a larger phrase, without further designation of its character. Again Marcion, as far as we know, made no particular claim to γνῶσις; and a word less characteristic of his teaching could hardly have been chosen. Once more, it is impossible to refer this phrase to Marcion and also other language of these Epistles to Valentinian or other similar teaching: the two suppositions exclude each other, but are in truth alike groundless. This seductive verbal coincidence being given up, there is nothing in what we know of Gnosticism, or of other speculative systems of the first two centuries, for which the term ἀντιθέσεις has any special appropriateness.

probably casuistical

'Ἀντιθέσεις has various possible meanings. The most obvious here would be one of those belonging to Greek rhetoric, 'objections' almost 'cavils'[1]. So Chrysostom here ἄρα εἰσὶν ἀντιθέσεις πρὸς ἃς οὐδὲ ἀποκρίνεσθαι δεῖ, and apparently Theodore of Mopsuestia. But the most probable is the simplest, nearly equivalent to our *antitheses*, the setting of one point against another. If we are still even here dealing with Jewish matter, a question which must wait till we come to τῆς ψευδωνύμου γνώσεως, ἀντιθέσεις, *oppositiones*, would seem an appropriate word to

[1] Cf. e.g. Philo, *Fragm.* ii. 634 Mang.

describe the endless contrasts of decisions[1], founded on endless distinctions, which played so large a part in the casuistry of the Scribes as interpreters of the Law. It would thus designate frivolities of what was called the Halacha, as the μῦθοι and γενεαλογίαι designate frivolities of the other great department of Jewish learning, the Haggada.

'Knowledge falsely so called' *Gnostic use of 'Gnosis'*

But how about the ψευδώνυμος γνῶσις? What is the most natural interpretation of this famous phrase?

Gnosis, in the sense of esoteric lore, was no doubt a favourite word and idea among the various sects whom we are accustomed to call Gnostics (γνωστικοί being however historically of much narrower application), though the application of it as a descriptive title of the whole movement, apart from this passage of 1 Tim., is modern only.

Pre-gnostic

Again, there are various traces of a similar use of the word before the Gnostics properly so called. In the Epistle of Barnabas it has an analogous sense, specially as a method of mystical interpretation of language and rites. So also Justin Martyr (*Dial.* 112, 339 C) writes, "There is nothing of what has been said or done by all the prophets without exception which can be justly plainer ἐὰν τὴν γνῶσιν τὴν ἐν αὐτοῖς ἔχητε." The reference is to the Brazen Serpent as a sign of Christ on the Cross.

e.g. vi 9 ix 8

Scriptural

But the truth doubtless is that it was a natural designation of any kind of lore that went below the

[1] See Weber, *Syst. d. alt. Syn. Pal. Theol.* 101 f. See Appendix.

surface of things, whatever might be the nature of the subject matter. The word itself is of tolerably frequent occurrence in LXX. (almost always for דַּעַת), Apocrypha, and New Testament.

Indirect evidence of special Jewish connotation

While then, taken by itself, it might be easily understood in various different ways, the question we have to ask is whether it would naturally be used of any Jewish lore not Gnostic in character, in accordance with the other indications in this Epistle.

from N. T.

Now the New Testament contains two or three places which at least indirectly bear on this question.

In Luke xi. 52 our Lord accuses the lawyers (τοῖς νομικοῖς) of having taken away the key of knowledge (τῆς γνώσεως). Here, as so often, He seems to be putting the true primary sense of a phrase in place of its conventional sense. It was their proper duty to open the door of knowledge for the people, that knowledge of realities human and Divine by which a man could be fitted for entrance into the kingdom of heaven. That true key however they took away by the barren traditionalism which they called knowledge, and of which they boasted themselves to hold the key[1].

So again in Rom. ii. 20 f. the boastful Jew is one who is confident that he is an instructor of the foolish,

[1] Cf. Rec. Clem. i. 54 Sed hi [Scribae et Pharisaei], baptizati a Johanne, et velut clavem regni caelorum verbum veritatis tenentes ex Moysis traditione susceptum, occultarunt auribus populi. Cf. ii. 30, 46; also Hom. Clem. xviii. 15 f.

a teacher of babes, which hath "the form of knowledge and of the truth in the law," where again St Paul seems to speak at once of a counterfeit *γνῶσις* and a true *γνῶσις* which had its *μόρφωσις* in the Law[1].

from LXX

Another indirect piece of evidence in the same direction is afforded by the way in which knowledge (*γνῶσις* LXX.) and Law correspond to each other in parallel clauses, cf. Hos. iv. 6; Mal. ii. 7.

'The Wise Men'

Lastly, a strong justification of this reference of *γνῶσις* is to be found in the common Jewish designation of the Scribes or Teachers of the Law. They were called the חֲכָמִים or wise ones; and it is noteworthy that while in Biblical Hebrew the verb חָכַם is always neuter, to be wise, in Rabbinical Hebrew and in Aramaic it is often transitive, answering exactly to *γινώσκω*, even in secondary senses of *γινώσκω*. If we could say for certain that the abstract substantive חָכְמָה (or other substantival form) were likewise used for *γνῶσις* in the corresponding sense, the proof would be obviously complete. I cannot however find evidence that such was the case. But since the common designation of the Scribes implied that they were men having knowledge quite as much as men having wisdom, the step to St Paul's presumed use of the word is but a small one. It is also worth notice that דַּעַת, which in the Old Testament is almost the

[1] Cf. 4 Mac. i. 16 f., *Σοφία δὴ τοίνυν γνῶσις θείων καὶ ἀνθρωπίνων πραγμάτων καὶ τῶν τούτων αἰτίων. αὕτη δὴ τοίνυν ἐστὶν ἡ τοῦ νόμου παιδεία δι' ἧς τὰ θεῖα σεμνῶς καὶ τὰ ἀνθρώπινα συμφερόντως μανθάνομεν.*

only original of the LXX. γνῶσις, in the Talmud sometimes means the sense of the Law in a particular case, or the opinion of this or that Rabbi on the sense of the Law[1]. Here again we have an easy transition, viz. from the single γνώσεις to their sum, the collective γνῶσις.

A little reflexion will shew that this would be quite a natural and legitimate application of the term γνῶσις. The distinctive lore of a class of canonists and casuists was in the strictest sense a special knowledge, a knowledge limited to experts or initiated persons; and this is the fundamental idea of γνῶσις in the quasi-technical sense with which we are concerned. It lies behind the familiar exclamation "This multitude which knoweth not the law (ὁ μὴ γινώσκων τὸν νόμον) are accursed"; an exclamation which has often been illustrated by Rabbinical language about the sharp line of demarcation between the Wise Ones and the Am Haaretz. Jn vii 49

Traces of 'dualism'

One other point remains to be noticed. A speculative dualism, a reluctance to recognise any contact between God and things divine on the one hand, and material and corporeal things on the other, is an important element both of Gnosticism and of other speculative systems; and it is said that 1 Tim. betrays the presence of a similar teaching at Ephesus.

[1] See examples in Levy-Fleischer i. 416. See illustrative Rabbinical examples of דעת in Weber, *u. s.* p. 24.

Future
1 Tim v 23

The most telling piece of evidence is of course the warning against "giving heed to deceiving spirits and to teachings of demons uttered by men speaking falsely in hypocrisy, having their own conscience branded, forbidding to marry or to partake of certain foods." As however we saw before, the teaching here spoken of is not present but future.

Practical
1 Tim iv 8

Again five verses lower St Paul addresses Timothy himself in a very different tone respecting bodily exercise, i.e. ἄσκησις, of which he speaks slightingly but not in condemnation.

1 Tim v 23

Similarly in the next chapter the injunction to him to be no longer a water-drinker is evidently, in the context in which it stands, not merely a sanitary but quite as much a moral precept, and thus implies that Timothy had himself begun to abjure wine on grounds of personal sanctity.

Met by positive teaching

Once more, despite the striking contrast in tone between the first passage and the second and third, there is unquestionably a real connexion between the first and the second. The positive teaching in iv. 4, 5 is evidently not simply laid down beforehand for a future time, but put forward as a necessary doctrine for the present, and thus implies that, as was to be expected, the germs of what would hereafter amount to a revolt from the faith (the faith of the Incarnation) (to be taught apparently by heathen oracles or other authorities of heathen religion, for such seems to be the meaning of "teachings of demons") were already to be found lurking under plausible forms; nay, that apparently Timothy himself had some need to be warned against them, at least so far as the matter of foods was concerned. The Christian teaching set up in *vv.* 4, 5 against the anticipated errors is itself according to *v.* 6 to be at once put before the brethren. 1 Tim iv 4 ff.

But not speculative. In all this there is no sign of a speculative kind of dualism. We have before us a practical ethical or religious teaching, a crude and hasty way of translating into action the true perception that for man in his present state all virtuous or godly life involves orderly restraint of the natural bodily desires. Such a rule of life may either rest on a speculative basis, as it did in much Platonic philosophy and in the Persian religion and Manicheism, or it may be independent of all such theoretical foundations. In the absence of more distinctive characteristics it is vain to try to determine the source of the tendencies here described.

Possibly Judaic in origin. For our purpose, however, it is natural to ask whether they came from the Judaism of Ephesus. Contempt for marriage was certainly not what we should look for in a Jewish community[1]. Simon Ben Azai's (Cent. II.) seclusion from his wife was evidently regarded[2] by the Rabbis as altogether exceptional. Yet it may have been otherwise with Jews of the

[1] Yet cf. Hebr. xiii. 4 [Ed.].

[2] Jost, *Gesch. d. Judenth.* ii. 97 ff.; Grätz, *Gnosticismus u. Judenthum* 71 ff.

Dispersion, peculiarly exposed to various foreign influences. It is remarkable that in the midst of this context St Paul bids Timothy avoid the profane and old wives' fables. In Titus i. 13 we hear distinctly of "Jewish fables" and that in connexion with "commandments of men". It cannot be proved that the *μῦθοι* in the two Epistles are of the same kind: but the presumption is that they are, more especially when
1 Tim i 4 the *μῦθοι* of an earlier place in this same Epistle had every appearance of being Jewish.

On the whole then in the Pastoral Epistles, no less than in Colossians, it seems impossible to find clear evidence of speculative or Gnosticising tendencies. We do find however a dangerous fondness for Jewish trifling, both of the legendary and of the legal or casuistical kind. We find also indications, but much less prominent, of some such abstinences in the matter of foods (probably chiefly animal food and wine) as at Colossæ and Rome, with a probability that marriage would before long come likewise under a religious ban. But of circumcision and the perpetual validity of the law we have nothing.

LECTURE VIII

James, 1 Peter, Hebrews, Apocalypse

FROM St Paul and the churches which he founded or to which he wrote we come back to the East. Of the remaining books of the New Testament, at least four belong to the decade preceding the Fall of Jerusalem. These four are the Epistles bearing the names of James, 1 Peter, Hebrews, and the Apocalypse embodying the Epistles to the seven Churches. All of them have some bearing, direct or indirect, on our subject, though in unequal degrees. They do not claim however more than a small part of our remaining time.

The Epistle of St James.

Authorship and Date

The Epistle bearing the name of James is still the subject of endless discussions. My own belief is first, that it is not the work of a late writer assuming wrongly the name of James but a true and authentic product of the apostolic age; and secondly that the

James who wrote it was the James of the latter part of the Acts, he who was known as the Lord's brother, not himself of the original Twelve but specially associated with them at Jerusalem, and the head of the local Church there. The apparent immaturity, as it were, of its teaching, together with other subordinate considerations, leads many who accept its genuineness to place it very early, at least as early as any Epistle of the New Testament. They are then obliged to assume that the whole of the famous passage on faith and works in ii. 14—26 has nothing to do with St Paul, and is to be explained by language found in Jewish writers. The passages hitherto adduced, however, do not appear to me to be adequate to support this theory so far as *vv.* 21—25 are concerned, and it seems more natural to suppose that a misuse or misunderstanding of St Paul's teaching on the part of others gave rise to St James's carefully guarded language. It follows that St Paul's controversy with the Judaizers, which for us is summed up permanently in Romans i—viii, must have preceded; and there is no tangible evidence at variance with this conclusion. Nay, the state of things which could lead to the writing of such a letter does not seem likely to have arisen very quickly. On the other hand, the latest limit is fixed by St James's death. Assuming the genuineness of

Ant. xx. ix. 1.

the passage relating to him in Josephus, and I see no good reason to question it, the events associated with it in Josephus's narrative fix it to the year 62; and though the vaguer language of Hegesippus, if it stood alone, would suggest a time nearer to the siege of Jerusalem by the Romans, it is not really at variance with this date. How long before St James's death the Epistle was written, we cannot tell: but the evident growth of persecution implied in the first and last sections suggests a late rather than a relatively early year.

Eus. *H.E.* ii. 23.

e.g. i 2; v 10

Recipients

The recipients of the Epistle according to i. 1 are "the twelve tribes that are in the Dispersion," and this very full phrase unaccompanied by words suggesting another than the literal meaning cannot naturally be understood except of Jews; while other passages shew Christian Jews, and apparently these alone, to be intended. Here and everywhere in the Epistle the Gentiles are neither included nor excluded; they are simply left out of account. If it was true to say that they were equal members of the new Israel of God, it was no less true to say, as St Paul and St John likewise virtually say, that Christian Jews were now the only true and adequate members of the ancient Israel, the faithful remnant, in prophetic language, in the midst of 'faithless and disobedient' members of the same people. Additional emphasis is given to this conception by *ταῖς δώδεκα φυλαῖς*, which signifies the ideal unbroken unity of the people[1]. The geographical compre-

[1] Cf. τὸ δωδεκάφυλον in Acts xxvi. 7; Clem. Rom. 55; *Protev. Jac.* 1.

hensiveness of the address would in the full doubtless be hardly carried out in the actual destination of the Epistle. But the homeward return of Jews, probably including Jewish Christians, who had come from distant lands to Jerusalem for the Pentecostal or another feast, would afford St James an opportunity of diffusing his letter widely enough; and it was natural and fitting that he, as the acknowledged head of the Church of Jerusalem, should send this word of exhortation and encouragement under trying circumstances to those Christians throughout the empire whose earlier religion had been not heathen but Jewish. It does not follow however that we can learn much respecting Jewish Christians of the Dispersion from the Epistle. It is not even safe to assume that they formed distinct congregations from those of Gentile Christians. Thus in ii. 2 (*ἐὰν γὰρ εἰσέλθῃ εἰς συναγωγὴν ὑμῶν ἀνὴρ χρυσοδακτύλιος* etc.) St James's appeal would have none the less force if Gentile Christians were worshippers in the same congregation; and the term *συναγωγή* is that which St James from his Palestinian experience would naturally and rightly use even if some or all of the congregations to which the recipients of the letter belonged were called not *συναγωγαί* but *ἐκκλησίαι*. In v. 14 *τοὺς πρεσβυτέρους τῆς ἐκκλησίας* is even a less distinctive phrase. Again, as regards the social conditions and moral evils to which the Epistle refers, it is not necessary to suppose that St James had an exact knowledge of the condition of the various Christian Churches of the Dispersion, which doubtless differed much from each other in important circumstances. The primary picture seems rather to be reflected from his own experience of the state of things at Jerusalem, which he knew was likely in one form or another to reproduce itself wherever Jews were to be found, whether they had become Christian Jews or not.

Characteristics of Teaching

For our purpose it is sufficient to cast a glance at some features of St James's own teaching. Unlike as it is on the surface to that of the other books of the New Testament, it chiefly illustrates Judaistic Christianity by total freedom from it. We find not a word breathing the spirit which chafed at St Paul's gospel to the Gentiles. We do not find even a temporary veneration for the as yet unabolished sanctities of Jewish ritual or polity. The echoes of the Sermon on the Mount have been often noticed: but what especially concerns us to observe is how deeply St James has entered into that part of the Sermon on the Mount which we examined at the outset, the true manner of the fulfilment of the Law. The Law itself in a true sense stands fast: but this (Ja ii 10 f.) permanence belongs to that in it which has the nature of a perfect law, a law of liberty, a royal law. Nay, just as our Lord appealed from the Mosaic (Mt xix 8) legislation to the Divine word spoken "from the beginning," as the utterance as it were of the Law within and behind the Law, so various sayings of St James, rightly understood, carry us back to the primary creation in the Divine image as the true standard of a right life; and thus implicitly lead the way to the restoration of the Divine image which is made possible by the Gospel.

e.g. i 23 iii 9

His traditional asceticism

The doctrinal position thus assumed involves however no necessary contradiction to the position which he is said to have held among the Jews at the time of his death. It is likely enough that recent critics are right in conjecturing that some features in the well-known striking narrative of Hegesippus preserved by Eusebius were borrowed from the Ebionite book called Ἀναβαθμοὶ Ἰακώβου mentioned by Epiphanius, from which parts of the first book of the Clementine Recognitions were also apparently borrowed. This identification indeed presupposes that the ἀναβαθμοί meant are the steps of the temple; whereas Epiphanius seems to me to understand the word figuratively, as it were steps in teaching, instructions: but it is not at all clear that he had ever seen the book himself, so that he may easily have misunderstood the title. Now it is likely enough that its contents were either largely or wholly fictitious. But we have no right to assume that this was the only source of information respecting St James used by Hegesippus, though it is difficult or impossible to distinguish precisely whence each of his statements came. But the general picture which he

Eus. *H.E.* ii. 23.

Hær. xxx. 16.

draws of St James's sanctity after a Jewish pattern, and of the veneration felt for him by his countrymen, is practically supported by the testimony of Josephus, assuming the passage from the last book of his Antiquities to be genuine. Most of the details merely go to shew that St James lived under a permanent Nazirite vow. This is not more surprising than St Paul's temporary vow or vows: and this whole representation of the life of the most prominent Christian Jew in Jerusalem is, to say the least, fully consistent with what might be expected in one holding that position while the Jewish commonwealth remained apparently unshaken. Nothing had yet occurred to make it an anachronism. The progress of the Pauline Gospel among the Gentiles, however heartily it might be welcomed by St James and his wiser associates, was but an additional reason why he should conspicuously maintain that retrospective aspect of the whole truth of God of which he was by his very position the appointed representative.

The First Epistle of St Peter

We come next to St Peter and his great Epistle. In Gal. ii. 7 he is said to have been recognised as entrusted with the Gospel of the Circumcision as St Paul was of the Uncircumcision. This was apparently, as we have seen, at the private conversations which preceded the great public conference at Jerusalem about the circumcision of Gentile converts.

Commission not limited to 'the Circumcision' The same is virtually repeated two verses on, when Peter (as 'Cephas') stands between James and John. This passage however gives us but one side of St Peter's function. In St Luke's account of the public

Ac xv 7 conference he stands forward to commend Paul and Barnabas and their mission to the assembly, avowedly as being himself the man, through whom the Gentile Cornelius had been Divinely admitted into fellowship. The actual counsel adopted by the assembly, whoever may have privately suggested it beforehand, comes formally from the mouth of St

Ac xv 14 James, who begins by ratifying St Peter's significant appeal to the past. After that verse St Peter's name disappears from the Acts. The New Testament gives us no information about the transition in the work of the Twelve between that day at Jerusalem and the much later times when we find St Peter writing his Epistle and St John his Apocalypse. As however we saw at the outset, the Twelve were from the first Divinely commanded to preach to the Gentiles. Through long years they felt it their duty, equally in obedience to Divine commands, to make the Holy City and Land their sphere of labour: but after a while they were bound to go forth. St Paul's intervening work may well have changed their whole horizon; but it had not superseded their own duty. Under what circumstances the great change took place, we have unfortunately no knowledge.

To this latter period of the work of the Twelve,

having its predominant character inexorably determined by the work and life of St Paul, as well as by our Lord's monitions, St Peter's Epistle belongs. He writes as one whose commission is universal: the local circumstances of the Church of Jerusalem or of any other Church cannot limit his action or his view. Nay, writing, as I believe he does, from Rome, the centre of the Empire, his momentary local position itself gives additional power to the universality of his teaching. Like St James, and yet more than St James, he writes to admonish and encourage Christians suffering under persecution. Their Churches were doubtless predominantly formed from heathen converts: yet he treats them as sharers in the ancestral prerogatives of Israel; and that not by an afterthought, as it were, of the Divine Will, but in accordance with the Divine purpose as it existed before the beginning of things. He teaches them the truth of the meaning of suffering in the person of Messiah, first suffering and then glorified; the object of anticipation to the Old Testament prophets who had likewise declared God's coming grace to reach to all mankind; the true Paschal Lamb whose blood had purchased their deliverance from old heathen bondage. He teaches them likewise to regard themselves as belonging to a people which inherits the ancient promises and glories of Israel, an elect race, a royal priesthood. Here therefore, as in the Epistle to the Ephesians, all that Palestinian

Treats Gentiles as sharers in the prerogative of Israel

1 Pet i 2

1 Pet i 11

1 Pet i 10

1 Pet i 18f.

1 Pet ii 9

Christianity represented is entirely out of sight. There is no trace of transitional conditions, in which the letter of the old Law and Covenant has still a certain legitimacy. The Israel of the future is the only Israel in view.

The Epistle to the Hebrews

The Address of the Letter

With the Epistle to the Hebrews we return again to Palestine. Such at least is I feel sure the true address of this mysterious epistle. There was a time when Egypt, with the temple of Leontopolis for a sacred centre, was regarded by many critics as the land for which it was written, and this view has eminent defenders still. Just now, Rome is still more a favourite, and that with excellent critics of very different schools. But, in spite of the difficulties suggested by the language of some individual verses, it seems to me morally impossible that the circumstances of the Jewish Christians addressed were the circumstances of any part of the Dispersion: in other words the great part of the Epistle would have been, as far as our knowledge goes, beside the mark if written to any region but Jerusalem and Judea. The Epistle of St James and that to the Hebrews are full of striking contrasts, in part no doubt owing to differences of temperament and position between the two writers; but owing likewise to the fact that the one was written to Christian Jews of the Dispersion and the other to Christian Jews of Palestine.

Dangers to faith in Palestine

The religious condition of these Jewish Christians shews plainly the dangers to faith which inevitably beset that form of Jewish Christianity which we have seen to have been legitimate in Palestine, the adoption of the Gospel without any disuse of the Law. It was only for a time that such a combination could be legitimate, and now the hour was at hand when it could be legitimate no longer. Meanwhile, before the announcement of the hour by the trumpet of Divine judgments, the mere force of long-continued custom had rendered possible a state of things which threatened to destroy all reality in men's allegiance to the Gospel. The freshness of power with which it had at first laid hold on them had died away, while the deep-seated instincts of ancestral custom preserved all their tenacious influence, and were aided by the corresponding spiritual degeneracy which made a religion of sight easier, and apparently more substantial, than a religion of faith. Then it would seem that the pressure of the unbelieving Jews, in the midst of whom the Jewish Christians were living, was now becoming heavier and more intolerable, in great measure, doubtless, owing to the unrest caused by the signs of approaching Roman invasion. Thus, without abjuring the name of Jesus, His professed followers in Palestine were to a large extent coming to treat their relation to Him as trivial and secondary compared with their relation to the customs of their forefathers and their living countrymen, and to

Heb x 25 give up that gathering together in Christian congregations which gave outward expression and inward reality to membership in the true people of God and of His Christ. We hear nothing about circumcision, and nothing about Gentile Christians. The Christianity here rising may be justly called a Judaistic Christianity; but it was rather the product of a degeneracy in heart and mind than the expression of a conscious doctrine or theory.

The transitoriness of the Law

If we compare the course followed by the author of the Epistle with the lines of thought which we have already met with in the Gospels and in the Apostolic age, it is remarkable that we find nothing of that idea of an essential permanence of the Law in virtue of the fulfilment of its Divine purpose which is laid down in the Sermon on the Mount. Though the writer has given Levitical observances a kind of prominence entirely absent in the rest of the New Testament, the Law is to him a thing that passes away altogether and is succeeded by something wholly better, the
Heb x 1 substance of which the Law was but the shadow. In other words, his teaching resembles that of the second set of passages in the Gospels, that set to which the language used respecting John the Baptist belongs. Twice indeed he quotes the great passage of Jeremiah on the new covenant which includes among other things the promise that God will give His laws in men's hearts and write them on their minds. But, though, like St James, he never uses the word Gospel

or the verb connected with it, he is not for that reason led to use such language as St James's about a Law which is in fact one aspect of the Gospel under another name, a glorified and evangelic Law. His choice of subjects for arguments is apparently guided not by any theoretical considerations, but by a sense of the influences which were as a matter of fact most potent with the Hebrew Christians. Priesthood, sacrifices, ancient covenant, commonwealth, these were the chief things that seemed substantial and solid beside the Christian realities that were losing their power of attraction; and therefore he dwells on their inexorably transitory nature, while he points out that each would pass away only to give place to something better than itself. To what extent the writer invites the Hebrew Christians to separate themselves by their own act from their unbelieving countrymen is not clear, even from xiii. 13. But at least he bids them accept the position without the camp. To be joined to Him who was the Author Heb xii 2
and Finisher of their faith was primary and essential; to be joined to priesthood and sacrifices, to ancient covenant and commonwealth, was secondary and not essential: before long it would be impossible, already it might be becoming wrong.

The Apocalypse

The day of the Lord which the writer to the Hebrews saw drawing nigh had already begun to break in blood and fire when St John sent his Apocalypse to the Gentile Churches of Asia. It is to be hoped that the drastic criticism which this difficult book has lately been receiving will have the indirect effect of ultimately throwing light on the still obscure historical circumstances under which it was written; and on the question whether events specially affecting the Palestinian Church, in addition to the Fall of Jerusalem, are to be included among the historical circumstances implied in its language. Meanwhile its special interest for our purpose is the testimony which, when carefully read, it bears to that Apostolic view of the relations of the Christian Church to Judaism which we have found in St Paul, St Peter, and in the Epistle to the Hebrews.

No traces of Jewish exclusiveness

The ἡμᾶς of i. 5, 6 (and again v. 10) can be none but Christians. Of these St John says that "Jesus Christ, the witness (or Martyr) who is true, the first-born of the dead and the ruler of the kings of earth, who loveth them and had ransomed them from their sins at the price of His own blood, had also made them to be a kingdom, priests to His God and Father." Here the words "a kingdom, priests" are taken from the words which Moses at Sinai was

Ex xix 6 to speak on the part of Jehovah to the people of

Israel, and which in another (the LXX) translation are applied by St Peter to the new Israel of Asia Minor. 1 Pet ii 9

in the New Jerusalem So also in chap. xxi. the vision of New Jerusalem recalls the language of the last chapters of Hebrews, as well as of Gal. iv. 26, cf. Phil. iii. 20. Heb xii 22

The inscription of the names of the twelve tribes on the portals, and of the names of the twelve apostles of the Lamb on the foundations of the wall must not mislead us into fancying that we have here a Judaistic dream. This city without a temple bears no sign of Jewish limitation. The recurring twelve is but a sign that under the Old and New Covenants alike, God had His one people, His true Israel, at first limited to one nation, afterwards bought out of every tribe and tongue and people and nation. The twelve apostles had of course reference in the first instance to the theoretical twelve tribes of the earthly Israel: but their original function, as we have seen to have been ordained by our Lord Himself, extended to the Gentiles likewise; and in actual history St Peter and St John, the only two of the twelve of whom we have any clear knowledge in the later Apostolic age, became at last teachers of the Gentiles. Thus as a band of twelve the apostles are specially significant representatives of the continuity between the old and the new Israel. (Ap xxi 12; Ap xxi 14; Ap xxi 22)

or in the sealing of the Tribes If then we turn back to the double vision of ch. vii, the voice of the angel respecting the sealing of the Ap vii 4, 9

12,000 out of every tribe, and then the sight of the great multitude whom no one could number, out of every nation and tribes and peoples and tongues, we cannot but feel the incongruity introduced by the plausible interpretation which makes the 144,000 to be Jewish Christians, and the great multitude Gentile Christians. The difficulty is increased by the total absence of any other sign of prerogatives ascribed to Jewish Christians as such in the book, directly or by implication, to say nothing of the absence of any signs of a corresponding difference of status in other books of the New Testament. Whatever then be the true interpretation, this one at least can hardly be true. When however we observe that in the first vision nothing is described as *seen* except the angel, his cry of prohibition to the other four angels, and the number of the sealed, being only *heard*, not seen, one cannot but suspect that the 144,000 spoken of and the great multitude seen may be one and the same body, Jewish Christians and Gentile Christians alike. As spoken of by the angel, they may be described under an exact ideal numeration[1] as making up the ideal Israel: as seen by the prophet they may be presented in accordance with external fact as a vast mixed multitude. But however this may be, the sealing of the twelve tribes cannot be recognised as a mark of Jewish exclusiveness.

or in the Epistles to the Churches

These are for our purpose the most important

[1] Cf. Hermas *Sim.* ix. 17. 1 f. See Appendix.

passages of the book. But it is worth while to notice in the Epistles to Smyrna and Philadelphia the language about "them who say that they themselves are Jews, and are not, but they lie," evidently aimed at unbelieving Jews, whom by reason of their unbelief the apostle regards as having forfeited the glories of their race. This is precisely the idea which St Paul expresses in Rom. ii. 28, 29. Less clear is the analogous sentence in the Epistle to Ephesus, about "them who call themselves apostles, and they are not, and thou didst find them false". It would be unprofitable to waste words on the strange theory that St Paul is meant by these false apostles: and it is very doubtful whether from any other point of view the interpretation of the words falls within our subject.

Ap ii 9; iii 9

Ap ii 2

We have now come to the end of the evidence of the New Testament, so far as it seems profitable to pursue it. It is better to keep clear of the faint and disputable illustrations of our subject which might conceivably be obtained from enquiries into the origin and purpose of each of the four Gospels and of the Acts; nor is anything substantial for our purpose to be gained from the remaining Epistles. It is on the other hand full time to enter on the history which lies outside the New Testament.

LECTURE IX

The Church of Jerusalem from Titus to Hadrian

St James's Epistle took us just now to St James's death and the picture of him preserved by Eusebius from Hegesippus, partly to all appearance derived from the lost Ebionite book called the *Steps of James*. Hegesippus is likewise our authority for nearly all of the little that we know of the fortunes of the Palestinian Church for a generation or two longer.

Eus. *H. E.* ii. 23.

Hegesippus

Was he a Judaizer?

Hegesippus, who belongs to the latter half of the Second Century, stands in an interesting relation to our subject both in modern theory and in undoubted historical fact. Not long ago in the eyes of a powerful body of critics he was the most striking representative of the Judaistic Christianity of the Second Century, and this view is still in substance upheld by some. In this instance a plausible case undoubtedly existed, and it was only by a more comprehensive view of the facts and probabilities that it could be set aside. It rested not only on the ample evidence that he had special knowledge of Palestinian Christianity but also on the telling fact that he was apparently recorded as having exclaimed against words of St Paul, viz. "Eye hath not seen nor ear heard," etc. Since however it is credibly attested that similar words occurred in an apocryphal writing, now lost, it is but reasonable to suppose that this, not 1 Corinthians, is the source of the quotation to which Hegesippus opposed the Lord's words "Blessed are the eyes that see, etc.," since otherwise there is a hopeless contradiction with known facts about Hegesippus. Moreover Stephen Gobar, the Sixth Century writer who mentions the criticism, does not give St Paul's name, but uses a vague plural (τοὺς ταῦτα φαμένους). 1 Cor ii 9

His knowledge of Palestine

The evidence that he had a special acquaintance with Palestinian Christianity is of several kinds. (1) The various particulars of its history which Eusebius recounts on his authority; (2) the statement of Eusebius that "he makes citations from the Gospel according to the Hebrews and the Syriac Gospel, and specially (or separately, ἰδίως) from the Hebrew language (i.e. apparently detached Hebrew words), thereby shewing himself to have been a believer of Hebrew origin, and moreover he mentions other matters as derived from Jewish unwritten Eus. *H. E.* iv. 22.

tradition"; and we may add (3) a bit of local knowledge apparently of an ocular kind, a statement at the end of his account of St James's martyrdom, "and they buried him on the spot beside the sanctuary, and his στήλη (monumental stone) still remains beside the sanctuary." It is not necessary to assume that a *stele* had been there ever since St James's death: but there was one in Hegesippus's time, and apparently he had seen it.

His visit by Corinth to Rome

What seems to be the best account of Hegesippus is Weizsäcker's rewritten article for the second edition of Herzog's *Encyclopädie*. He there points out the improbability of the common assumption based on Jerome's misunderstanding of Eusebius, that Hegesippus was an historian, and shews that his book (called ὑπομνήματα, 'Notes' or 'Memoirs'), was apparently a somewhat discursive controversial work against the heresies of his day[1]. The account of St James was, we learn, in the fifth or last book, which would be impossible if the work were a consecutive narrative of events. The only event that we know of in his life is a journey by Corinth to Rome: but what is said of these two places suffices to stamp his ecclesiastical character. For the purpose, it would seem, of his argument, he quoted much from Clement of Rome's Epistle to the Corinthians, and then in that connexion spoke of his own visit to Corinth. "And the Church of the Corinthians," he says, "continued

Eus. *H. E.* iv. 22.

[1] Cf. Westcott, *N. T. Canon*, p. 207 f.

in the right doctrine (τῷ ὀρθῷ λόγῳ) down to the time when Primus was Bishop in Corinth; with whom (plural) I had intercourse on a voyage to Rome, and spent with the Corinthians several days, during which we had restful sympathy with the right doctrine (συνανεπάημεν[1] τῷ ὀρθῷ λόγῳ)." This "right doctrine" must of course have been in harmony with that of Clement's Epistle, which we can see for ourselves to have had nothing Judaistic in it. Then he goes on to say how after his arrival at Rome he made out or procured a διαδοχή, apparently a list[2] of the successive bishops, down to Anicetus, who was apparently bishop at the time. "And in every succession," he says, "and in every city there is such a state of things as the Law proclaims and the Prophets and the Lord."

conclusive against Judaizing

This last phrase used to be cited as evidence of Hegesippus's legalism; but (as Ritschl[3] pointed out long ago) it is no more than the usual Second Century formula of Church writers to express the harmony of Old and New Testament against such heretics as rejected the Old Testament. It is true "the Apostles" are *generally* added, but their testimony

[1] It is possible that ἐν may have been lost after συνανεπάημεν. In any case the verb is from Rom. xv. 32.

[2] This list, as Lightfoot shewed in a letter to the *Academy* of May 21, 1887, is probably the list followed by Epiphanius (*Hæres.* xxvii. 6) who seems in this passage to be citing loosely from Hegesippus. See *Epp. of S. Clem.* I. p. 327 ff.

[3] *Ents. d. Alt. Kir.* p. 268.

might easily be regarded as included in that of the Lord; and indeed, as Westcott[1] has pointed out, the probably contemporary Epistles to Virgins which bear Clement's name have exactly the same form. Thus certainly at Corinth and at Rome and in other Churches, if he visited other Churches (ἑκάστῃ above is ambiguous), Hegesippus found himself in harmony with the authorities of the Church; and what is said of Clement's Epistle makes it impossible to suppose that this was a harmony in Judaistic doctrine or practice.

How can a Palestinian have escaped Judaizing?

How then are we to explain Hegesippus's special acquaintance with Palestinian Christianity? If he was brought up in it, should we not expect him, it might be asked, to shew at least some Judaistic tendency? No certain answer is possible for want of knowledge about Palestinian Christianity and for want of knowledge about Hegesippus. Whether Palestinian Christianity a generation or two before him was of necessity Judaistic, we shall have to ask just now. And again, we know, and evidently Eusebius knew, nothing about Hegesippus except what has been already mentioned: even his Jewish origin is apparently a matter of inference to Eusebius (ἐμφαίνει), not of knowledge. It is no doubt conceivable that long before he wrote he had passed from one form of the Christian faith to another. But it is to be remembered that the Church of Aelia,

[1] *N. T. Canon*, p. 187.

the Jerusalem of his day, was a Gentile Church, evidently in communion with other great Churches, as is shewn by the references to its Bishop Narcissus, his contemporary. Even if the continuity of local tradition was broken by the results of the war of Barcochba, to which we must soon come, some traditions of the earlier time were likely to survive among the descendants of the earlier Church on the other side of Jordan, not very many hours distant from Jerusalem, and an Aelian Christian of active mind would have little difficulty in gathering them up. The use of the native languages attested by Eusebius is not quite so easily explained in this way, though the example of Jerome shews that the supposition would not be extravagant. We shall come presently to a third explanation of the way in which Hegesippus may have become acquainted with the Palestinian traditions which have to be considered next. Howsoever they may have reached him, there is no reason to doubt that he faithfully reproduced them.

Eus. *H. E.* v. 23.

Eus. *H. E.* iv. 22.

Extracts from Hegesippus preserved in Eusebius

Eusebius *H. E.* iii. 5—10 is taken up with an account of the siege and fall of Jerusalem, expressly derived from Josephus, and then with an account of Josephus's writings and Canon.

Then in ch. 11 he proceeds:

The election of Symeon

"After the martyrdom of James and the immediately succeeding capture of Jerusalem it is recorded (λόγος κατέχει) that the survivors among the Apostles and the Lord's disciples met together from all quarters, along with those who were related to the Lord by blood, for many of these too were still alive : and that the whole number took counsel together as to whom they should adjudge worthy to succeed to James, and then that with one mind they all approved Symeon the son of Clopas, who is also mentioned by the Scripture of the Gospel, to be worthy of the throne of that see, being, as they say, a cousin of the Saviour. That is (γὰρ οὖν), Hegesippus relates that Clopas was a brother of Joseph. And further, that Vespasian gave orders after the capture of Jerusalem for inquisition to be made for all of the kindred of David, to the end that no one of the blood royal might be left alive among the Jews; and that the Jews on that account underwent yet another severe persecution."

Λόγος κατέχει is in itself a vague phrase; but as used by Eusebius, it by no means indicates that he had no precise authority. Thus in ch. 18 after using it he shews that he was following Irenæus. So here I feel sure that he is following Hegesippus, whom he does actually quote in a parenthesis at the end of ch. 11 for the fact of Clopas's relationship. In a modern writer we might suppose that this one accessory fact alone came from Hegesippus; but that is not Eusebius's manner. The description of the capture of Jerusalem as 'immediately succeeding' the martyrdom of James is probably due to the phrase, that not improbably came just before in Hegesippus, '*καὶ εὐθὺς Οὐεσπασιανὸς πολιορκεῖ αὐτούς*.' This phrase (preserved by Eusebius ii. 23, § 18) was used (as we have seen) in a rhetorical way by

Hegesippus, but it has been taken literally by Eusebius, who is thus misled into the incredible statement that the appointment of Symeon to succeed James took place after the fall of the city.

Jude's grand-children

The narrative is then, as often, interrupted by successions of Emperors (Titus succeeding Vespasian, Domitian Titus) and of Bishops. The mention of Clement as Bishop of Rome leads to an allusion (ch. 16) to Hegesippus's notice of the disturbance in the Church of Corinth in Clement's time. Domitian's reign leads to Domitian's persecution and St John's alleged banishment in it, and then (ch. 19) to an account by Hegesippus (introduced at first by *παλαιὸς κατέχει λόγος*), carrying on the former account of Vespasian's policy, how Domitian ordered the destruction of David's descendants. Then follows (ch. 20), doubly attested as from Hegesippus, the touching story of Jude's grandchildren, who were accused by 'certain heretics' to Domitian as coming under this description, and their release after his interview with them: after which they are said *ἡγήσασθαι τῶν ἐκκλησιῶν*, as being at once martyrs and of the Lord's kindred, and that, peace then coming and lasting till the reign of Trajan they survived till that time (§ 8).

Heresies rise after Symeon's Martyrdom

Eus. *H. E.* iii. 32.

Having reached the reign of Trajan in ch. 21, Eusebius is led to speak of St John's old age, and then, after some natural digressions, returns in ch. 32 to the ordinary course of his narrative, and on the authority of Hegesippus (preluded by κατέχει λόγος) mentions various local and popular persecutions of Christians in Trajan's reign, in one of which Bishop Symeon suffered martyrdom: here again 'certain heretics' appear (§ 3) as the accusers, and the accusation is twofold, of Davidic origin and of being a Christian. The accusers themselves in their turn are said (§ 4) to have been taken, as being of the tribe of Judah. Further on in the chapter after a repetition at somewhat greater length of the story of Jude's grandchildren we read (§ 7) that Hegesippus marks this as the time when the Church, hitherto free and inviolate, began to suffer from the open injury of those who endeavoured to corrupt "the sound rule of the saving message," any previous heretics having been secret and obscure. The allusion here is probably to Thebuthis, mentioned by Hegesippus as having begun to cause corruption because he had not been made bishop when Symeon was. He is said[1] to have been "of the seven sects," apparently not the sects next mentioned (§ 5), but the seven Jewish sects mentioned a little further on (§ 6). Apparently (ch. 32 § 8) he regarded the death of Symeon as the passing away of the last survivor of eye-witnesses of the Lord during whose lifetime error could not openly hold up its head.

Eus. *H. E.* iv. 22.

The succession of Justus

On the other hand, three chapters on, Pliny's

[1] The passage is corrupt, but the MSS. are certainly right in ὤν)(ὧν of the editors.

correspondence and an episcopal succession having intervened, we read, that at this time a vast number (μυρίων ὅσων) of the circumcision believed in Christ (the perfect πεπιστευκότων is ambiguous, but hardly the context), one of whom Justus (called Ἰουδαῖός τις) succeeded to Symeon. No authority is given, but it can be only Hegesippus. Eus. *H. E.* iii. 35.

With iv. 3 a new reign begins, that of Hadrian. After a few lines we come to episcopal successions at Rome and Alexandria. *List of Bishops in Jerusalem*

"But of the Bishops in Jerusalem," says Eusebius, "I have quite failed to find the dates preserved in writing; it is in fact (γὰρ οὖν) barely recorded (λόγος κατέχει) that they were short lived, but this much I have received from written sources, that till the siege of the Jews under Hadrian there had been fifteen Bishops in succession there, who, they say, were all Hebrews and had from the first received the knowledge of the Christ in its genuine form, so that they had been already approved by those who were competent to decide on such points as worthy of the Episcopal office; for their whole Church was composed of believing Hebrews, survivors from the time of Apostles even to that siege in which the Jews were overcome after severe fighting in their second revolt against Rome. Seeing then that the succession of Bishops of the Circumcision came to an end at that time it will be right to give a list of them from the beginning."

Then after the list[1] he continues:

"Such then is the number of the Bishops of the city of Jerusalem, extending from the time of the Apostles to the time indicated. All of these were of the Circumcision."

[1] This list is perhaps not from Hegesippus, but from Jerusalem registers. Cf. Eus. *Dem. Evang.* IV. 5. 124 D ὧν καὶ τὰ ὀνόματα εἰς ἔτι νῦν παρὰ τοῖς ἐγχωρίοις μνημονεύεται.

We have thus reached a point little if at all inferior in interest for our purpose to the Capture of Jerusalem by Titus, viz. the disastrous end of the war of Barcochba arising out of the substitution of the Gentile Aelia for the Jewish Jerusalem. Up to this time, we are told, there had been a quick succession of bishops from the circumcision, while they were also men whose faith in the opinion of Hegesippus was of the right stamp. The two facts have to be taken together.

The migration to Pella.

Before considering this point further, let us leave the Jerusalem Bishops and retrace our steps to the time of the first Roman conquest. In the chapter in which Eusebius describes the beginning of the great war entrusted to Titus, after enumerating the Jewish assaults on the Christian Community, especially the deaths of Stephen, James the son of Zebedee, and James the Lord's brother, and the departure of the other apostles to go forth among the Gentiles, because, he says, they were driven forth by plots against their life, he mentions further (§ 3) that "the people of the church in Jerusalem, by a certain oracle given by revelation τοῖς αὐτόθι δοκίμοις, had been ordered to remove before the war and inhabit Pella, a city of Peræa." He speaks of "those who had believed in Christ" having migrated from Jerusalem,

Eus *H. E.* iii. 5.

and of "holy men having entirely abandoned both the very royal metropolis of the Jews and the whole land of Judea." Then after this exordium he proceeds to the Divine judgment which fell on the guilty nation. Here there is no direct or indirect indication of authorship: but the contents suggest that at least the fact came from Hegesippus. It is difficult and not important to decide whether the time intended is at some pause between the first beginning of the war in May 66 A.D. and Titus's gathering of his army at Cæsarea in the spring of 70 A.D. or at that last crisis itself. Probably, however, it was at least late in the time. The country in which Pella lies was occupied by Vespasian in the spring of 68 A.D., a little before Nero's death, and the Christian colony, if then there, must have been swept away. The migration was doubtless connected with the supremacy gained by the Zealot party in Jerusalem and the tyranny which they exercised over the city. The natural effect of those terrible days would be that many of those Christians whose attachment to the Jewish state was stronger than their faith in the Gospel would become separated from the Church and lost in the mass of their countrymen. Thus the body which migrated to Pella would probably consist mainly of those who best represented the position formerly taken by St James, and those whom the teaching of the Epistle to the Hebrews had persuaded to loosen their hold on the ancient observances.

The time

The religious position of the emigrants

Heb xiii 13 This going forth was indeed literally a going forth without the camp, and the feelings with which the emigrants went forth must have been peculiarly in harmony with the Epistle; though the Epistle must have been written before so acute a crisis as this had been reached. The fact of the migration is nearly all that we really know about it. That Ebionite communities existed in that region in the Fourth Century is no evidence that they were descended from the fugitives from Jerusalem. Various other circumstances of less remote date might easily give rise to such communities.

Ariston's dogmatic position

One not improbable memorial of the time is the name of a writer whom Eusebius cites for a *H.E.* iv. 6, 3. decree of Hadrian respecting the Jews, Ἀρίστων ὁ Πελλαῖος. The same name is given by Maximus the Confessor (VII. Cent.) to the author of a Dialogue between Papiscus and Jason, a controversial work against the Jews which other ancient writers cite anonymously. Harnack[1] has shewn that there is every reason to suppose the same Ariston to be meant, and that the account of Hadrian's edict probably occurred in the Dialogue. It is of interest for our subject to note that Jason, the interlocutor who represents the author in this Dialogue, is called a Hebrew Christian, and yet that he is said to have vindicated *dispositionem* [οἰκονομίαν] *et plenitudinem Christi*, and that his interpretation

[1] *Texte und Unters.* Vol. I. pp. 115—130.

of Gen. i. 1 as preserved by Jerome, shews him to have held the Son of God to be pre-existent to the Creation; so that Ariston, the Christian of Pella, cannot have been a mere Ebionite.

The return from Pella

Epiphanius[1] speaks of the Christians as having returned from Pella to Jerusalem. It is in a parenthetic sentence in a long and curious story about Aquila the translator: but it is not required for the story, and was probably a conjectural addition by Epiphanius himself. Sooner or later, however, a more or less complete return from Pella to Jerusalem must have taken place, unless Hegesippus's whole account of the death of Symeon, and of the later bishops is a fiction, which is most unlikely.

Subsequent History.

According to the story in Epiphanius[2] in Hadrian's time, doubtless his early time, nothing was standing in Jerusalem except a few houses, the little Christian Church occupying the site of the room to which the apostles withdrew after the Ascension, parts of houses about Sion, and seven synagogues standing alone on Sion. Aquila also is said to have seen "the disciples of the disciples[3] of the apostles flourishing in the faith and working great signs of healings and other marvels." But the account has a very fantastic sound.

1 *De mens. et pond.* c. 15.

2 *loc. cit.* c. 14.

3 τοὺς μαθητὰς τῶν μαθητῶν. This is the reading of the Syriac. See P. de Lagarde, *Philologus*, xviii. p. 352.

Eusebius[1] seems at first sight to say that half the city only had been destroyed: but this apparently is only his deduction (εἰκός) from what he took to be a prophecy of the fate of Jerusalem in Zech. xiv. 2.

Relations between Jews and Christians in Palestine

Allusions in Jewish literature shew that at this time controversies between Jews and Christians were common[2], a Christian named Jacob (James) of Caphar Secania being oftenest named: but the quotations are strangely disappointing both as to their contents and as to geographical indication. One thing however is certain, that in this period the great seat of Jewish learning and mental activity was not Jerusalem but Jamnia near Joppa.

But there were other ways in which the Christians of Palestine must have been affected by the presence of their Jewish neighbours. Forty-six years after the destruction of Jerusalem by Titus a terrible insurrection of the Jews broke out, which included Palestine, though its chief rage was expended in Egypt, Cyrene, and Cyprus. In Cyprus alone 240,000 men are said to have been massacred by the Jews. A contest of this kind must, even more than the state of things during Titus's siege, have made an impassable chasm between the Jews and the Christians of Palestine, and made intermediate forms of belief and practice almost impossible. Then came the final war of Barcochba, when, exasperated by Hadrian's building up of

[1] *Dem. Evang.* vi. 18, 286 B.

[2] See Derenbourg, *Essai sur l'hist. et la géog. de la Palestine*, ch. xxi.

Jerusalem as a pagan city, and doubtless by other grievances, the Jewish martial frenzy burst out once more in a struggle which, says Mommsen[1], through its intensity and duration has no equal in the history of the Roman imperial period.

Expulsion of the Church of the Circumcision from Aelia

That one effect of the consequent sentence of expulsion against all Jews should lead to the banishment of the Christian community at Jerusalem is not strange, even if the old confusion between Christians and Jews had ceased. It was a church of the circumcision, and probably observed other Jewish rites, and so to the eye of a Roman it was a Jewish community. It may seem strange that these Jewish customs (not temple services) should be observed by Christians after Jerusalem had once fallen; and their retention was doubtless not only in spirit adverse to the Epistle to the Hebrews, but a real and really mischievous anachronism, not less at variance with the principles laid down by still greater authorities of the Apostolic age. But it may well have been that the cherished memory of St James may have led to an unintelligent copying of his policy under changed conditions; and Judaism itself was rapidly transforming the Law into a system of observances independent of temple or Holy City.

Its dogmatic position

That the Doctrine current in such a church would fall far short of that of any of the great apostles is probable enough: but the same may be said of every

[1] *The Provinces of the Roman Empire*, Eng. Tr. ii. 224.

church of that time of which we have any knowledge. This however would not justify our treating it as an essentially Ebionite Church, in the teeth of the reasonable interpretation of Hegesippus's words. What became of it after its expulsion by Hadrian, we know not. Probably enough it found some new Pella, one or many; and this seems to be on the whole the most probable solution of the question about Hegesippus's education. He may well have sprung from some city which harboured a part of the Jerusalem Church, and thus by birth, though not by locality, he would have its traditions for his own. And again, we have no reason to imagine that such a Christian society, holding fast the old Jerusalem faith, would be out of communion with the Church of Aelia, itself in communion with the other great Churches of Christendom: and if so, there is nothing anomalous in the ecclesiastical position implied in the extracts preserved by Eusebius. Such a supposition is fully in harmony with the language used by Justin Martyr in his *Dialogue*. Thus the general conclusion is that the Christianity of the Church of Jerusalem during the whole time between the unknown return from Pella and the war of Barcochba, and of the same Church in its probable subsequent transplantation to remoter parts of Judea, and of Hegesippus himself, were probably not Judaistic except to a certain extent in practice as distinguished from principle. The Ebionite or properly Judaistic bodies of Palestine will require separate consideration.

LECTURE X

THE JUDAIZERS OF THE IGNATIAN EPISTLES

BEFORE we pass to the consideration, indicated at the close of the last lecture, of the Ebionite or properly Judaistic bodies of Palestine, this is the most convenient place for saying a word on the Judaizers of the Ignatian Epistles, as a necessary appendix to our consideration of the Judaizers of the Epistles to the Colossians and the Pastoral Epistles. It is usual to treat the three subjects as forming a closely connected series, each illustrating and confirming the traditional interpretation of the others. As I have found myself constrained to question the Gnosticizing character of the two sets of teachers belonging to the apostolic age, it becomes incumbent on me not to pass over the corroborative evidence for it which is supposed to be afforded by the language of Ignatius.

Are the Judaizers here Docetic?

The facts are simply these. It is allowed on all hands that Ignatius refers to Docetic error and that he refers to Judaistic error. The question is whether these two forms of error were independent of each other or were held simultaneously by the same persons; on the latter supposition we have evidence here of a Docetic form of Judaistic Christianity; in the former we have none. Most critics, of different schools, believe the two forms of error to have been combined. In reading Zahn's admirable monograph on Ignatius some years ago, long before it had occurred to me that the current views as to the false teaching spoken of in the Epistle to the Colossians and the Pastoral Epistles rested on precarious grounds, I was struck with what seemed to me the weakness of Zahn's advocacy of this interpretation, and even Bishop Lightfoot's[1] clearer and more vigorous exposition of it has not convinced me to the contrary. Harnack[2], I am glad to see, likewise signifies (in a single sentence) that the Judaizers in Ignatius are distinct from the other false teachers. The polemic against Docetism is chiefly to be found in the Epistles to the Ephesians, and still more the Smyrnaeans and Trallians: that against Judaizing is confined to two, those to the Magnesians and Philadelphians.

The Judaizers in Magnesia
Magn. viii. 1.

The doctrinal warnings to the Magnesians begin *Μὴ πλανᾶσθε ταῖς ἑτεροδοξίαις μηδὲ μυθεύμασιν τοῖς παλαιοῖς ἀνωφελέσιν οὖσιν.* Here *ἑτεροδοξίαις* is an ambiguous word. If, as is quite possible, Ignatius is thinking of his Docetic antagonists, the *μηδέ* is to say

[1] *Epp. of Ign.* i. 359—375. [2] *Dogmengesch.* i. 225.

the least compatible with a transition to another party, in the next words, "Be not deceived by the ἑτεροδοξίαι, nor yet by the old fables which are unprofitable." 'Unprofitable' (apparently from Tit. iii. 9) would be a strangely weak word for grave doctrinal errors: nor could the term 'old' (παλαιοῖς) be applied in any intelligible sense to the μυθεύματα if, as is supposed, they were 'myths', relating to cosmogony and angelology: Jewish legendary lore is at least a more likely meaning, as in the Pastoral Epistles, from which however the phrase may be loosely borrowed in a vague way. He goes on "For if to this day we live in accordance with Judaism (or Jewish Law), we confess that we have not received grace."

Then comes a praise of the Prophets as having "lived in accordance with Christ Jesus; men who ἐν ch. ix.
παλαιοῖς πράγμασιν ἀναστραφέντες came to a newness of possession, no longer keeping sabbath but living according to the Lord's [day], on which also our life arose [out of death] through Him and His death, which [sc. the death] some deny." (This is doubtless a brief allusion to Docetic teachers, but it may as easily be a passing allusion as part of the polemic of these chapters.)

After a few lines on discipleship to Jesus Christ (ch. x.) he bids them put away the evil leaven which has grown old (παλαιωθεῖσαν) and sour, and turn to a fresh leaven, which is Jesus Christ. It is monstrous to "speak Jesus Christ" and to Judaize, for Christianism did not believe on Judaism, but Judaism on Christianism, which every tongue believing "was gathered unto God."

ch. xi. Finally, he says he had been warning them lest they should fall into the hooks of *κενοδοξία* (a quite ambiguous word, cf. the *κενοφωνία* of 1 and 2 Tim.), but "be ye fulfilled (*πεπληροφόρησθε*, i.e. as matured Christians) in the generation (*γέννησις*) and the passion and the resurrection which took place in the time when Pontius Pilate was governor:—things done truly and securely by Jesus Christ our hope." This last sentence is taken as proof that the Judaizing here spoken of was combined with Docetism: but it is just as likely that Ignatius in winding up with a description of the full ripe Christian faith falls naturally into his usual language about it.

Judaizers in Philadelphia Philad. v. So also in writing to the Philadelphians, having said that he has taken refuge with the Gospel as the flesh of Jesus, he goes on to associate with the Gospel Magn. viii. the Prophets (somewhat as in the other Epistle), and then in ch. vi. he contrasts with this true interpretation of the Prophets a false interpretation which some might bring before them. "But if any one interpret to you Judaism, hearken not to him, for it is better to hear Christianism from a circumcised man than Judaism from an uncircumcised" (implying, I suppose, by this curious antithesis, that a Jew might without inconsistency add to his Judaism Christianity, but that a Gentile Christian could not consistently adopt Jewish ways). cf. Magn. x.

Further on, in the course of the next two chapters, he apparently implies that these teachers had caused divisions, and it is to them that he probably refers as men who say "If I find it not in the archives [apparently the Old Testament] I believe not in the Gospel." "But to me," he replies "Jesus Christ is archives; His cross and Death and His resurrection and the faith that is through Him are the inviolable archives." "Good also," he adds (c. ix.) "are the [i.e. Jewish] priests, but better is the High Priest, who has been entrusted with the Holy of Holies, to whom alone have been entrusted the secrets of God, being Himself the Gate of the Father, through which enter in Abraham and Isaac and Jacob and the prophets and the Apostles and the Church. All these [sc. old and new] are unto the unity of God. But the Gospel has a certain special advantage, the *παρουσία* of our Saviour Lord Jesus Christ, His passion, His resurrection. For, the beloved Prophets *κατήγγειλαν εἰς αὐτόν*; but the Gospel is a completion (*ἀπάρτισμα*: cf. *πεπληροφόρησθε* in *Magn.* xi.) of incorruption." This climax shews the real *primary* force of the Magnesian climax, as in the first instance a contrast to the imperfection of the Old Dispensation. Philad. viii.

These are apparently the only passages in the Epistles which refer to Judaizing; and the only shadow of intermixture with the other form of error is in the two climaxes, already commented on, and the one allusion to the denial of Christ's death. They are both tolerably compact blocks, as it were, in the text. On the other hand the Docetic negations and the truth which they denied, the truth of the flesh and perfect humanity of Christ, haunt Ignatius almost incessantly. This fact amply accounts for that one reference to the denial of the Death, and likewise for some other references to Docetism in the first four chapters of the Epistle to the Philadelphians, which by no means overlap or intertwine with the subsequent language about Judaizing.

The Judaizing Pharisaic

The Law, Circumcision, and Sabbath, these are the only distinct marks of what Ignatius meant by Ἰουδαϊσμός in this connexion; that is, it appears to have been of the old simple Pharisaic type against which St Paul had to contend in Galatia, a region at no great distance from Philadelphia or even from Magnesia. If there be another element it is contained in that short phrase *μυθεύμασιν τοῖς παλαιοῖς* Magn. viii. *ἀνωφελέσιν οὖσιν*, which may either be, as the matter of the Pastoral Epistles would suggest, Haggadic legends of the patriarchs and the like; or else, by a *verbal* application of Tit. i. 14, Ἰουδαϊκοῖς *μύθοις καὶ ἐντολαῖς ἀνθρώπων ἀποστρεφομένων τὴν ἀλήθειαν*, a vague description of old-world Jewish precepts.

Docetism not necessarily Gnostic

It is likewise worth notice that the other false doctrine which Ignatius so persistently assails is simply Docetism; and that the common description of it as Gnosticism involves a large assumption. It is true that Docetism was an important element in various "Gnostic" systems, e.g. in that of Saturnilus of Antioch, with whose teaching Ignatius might easily have come in contact. But it is very doubtful whether conversely all Docetism had Gnostic accompaniments. We have in fact in the Apocryphal Acts of Apostles a large Docetic literature, to which the name "Gnostic" is with similar but more defensible looseness applied, and, in spite of the expurgated condition in which most of it has come down to us, we can see that the principal and perhaps only constant doctrinal accompaniment is a pseudo-asceticism especially condemnatory of marriage. Here no doubt we are reminded of the predictive passage of 1 Tim.: but then the Pastoral Epistles iv 1—3 apparently know nothing of Docetism; just as with the solitary exception of the *μυθεύματα*, the Ignatian Epistles know nothing of the supposed marks of Gnosticizing influences in the Pastoral Epistles. Even therefore if the two Ignatian forms of error met in the same teachers, we should doubtless have before us a very interesting, if startling, combination, but we should have in it no evidence illustrative of the Epistle to the Colossians or the Pastoral Epistles.

LECTURE XI

CERINTHUS. 'BARNABAS.' JUSTIN MARTYR.

Cerinthus

IF we were to include under Judaistic Christianity every ancient scheme of doctrine which comprised both Christian and Jewish elements, we should have to examine what can be known of Samaritan systems associated with the names of Simon Magus, Dositheus, Cleobius, and Menander. They are however of too eclectic a nature to fall properly under our subject. In another shape, as reflected in late fiction, Simon will come before us presently in connexion with the Clementine literature: but that is quite another matter. On the other hand we can hardly pass over Cerinthus, in spite of the difficulty of gaining a clear conception of his position; for he stands, to say the least, in closer relations to forms of belief strictly Judaistic.

His date His age, to start with, is curiously involved in

contradictions. According to the well known saying of Polycarp reported by Irenæus, twice quoted by Eusebius, he must have lived in St John's time, for St John was said to have fled out of the bath where he was. This early date would be supported or made earlier by the story which Epiphanius repeats, apparently from Hippolytus, that Cerinthus was the ringleader of St Paul's Judaizing antagonists at Jerusalem, if there were the slightest probability of its truth. On the other hand he stands by no means at the beginning in those lists of heretics which contain his name; and he is not mentioned at all by the earlier writers on heresies, Justin or Hegesippus (as far as we know), though the force of their silence is somewhat weakened by the equal silence of Clement and Tertullian later on. On the whole there is no sufficient reason to doubt the statement of Polycarp.

Iren. iii. 3. Eus. *H.E.* iii. 28. cf. iv. 14. *Hær.* xxviii. 4. Ac xxi 28

The earlier accounts, in accordance with this story, make Asia (i.e. the Roman province) the region of Cerinthus's activity: Hippolytus in his later work 'Against All Heretics' is silent about Asia, but makes him to have been trained in Egyptian lore, without however speaking of him as of Egyptian origin.

Hipp. *Hær.* vii. 33. cf. x. 21.

With the exception of a single point, all that we know of his doctrines seems to come from two sources, Irenæus[1] and the Syntagma of Hippolytus[2], and the two accounts do not altogether tally, even when we

[1] Cf. Irenæus i. 26, 1; iii. 11, 1.

[2] Cf. Lipsius, *Quellenkritik des Epiphanios* pp. 115—122.

iii. 11. have set aside one passage of Irenæus (p. 188), in which Valentinian and Cerinthian doctrines are mixed up together.

His doctrine

Our Lord, he taught, was the son of Mary and Joseph, born like other men. He inculcated circumcision and the sabbath. He rejected St Paul, the Acts, and all the Gospels except St Matthew's, which however he did not retain in its integrity. Thus far we have a type of Judaizing Christianity which was common enough. But with it he united Gnostic thoughts. According to Irenæus he said that Christ descended from above at the baptism on the Man Jesus (not however the *aeon* Christ, a designation which as regards Cerinthus is, I believe, a modern fiction), and revealed to Him the unknown Father and enabled Him to work miracles; and parted from him and flew up again before the Passion: according to the other account[1] a power from above (or the Holy Ghost) came similarly down on Christ.

He said that the Resurrection of Christ was still future. He taught that the world was made by angels, one of whom, the God of the Jews, gave the Jews their Law, which was not wholly good.

Eus. *H. E.* iii. 28. Last comes his strong and material form of Chiliasm, noticed by the Roman presbyter Gaius at the end of the third century, and by Dionysius of Alexandria half a century later. Chiliasm was however too

Eus. *H. E.* vii. 25.

[1] Hipp. *Omn. Hær. Ref.* vii. 33; Epiph. *Hær.* xxviii. 1.

widely accepted in the Second and Third Centuries among Christians quite free from Judaizing, for it to be safe to treat this as certainly coming from the Jewish side of Cerinthus's creed, even if it were certain that his doctrine was exceptionally material in character.

Here then we have at last a real instance of a Judaizing Christian, if indeed he can rightly be called a Christian, who was at the same time in the conventional sense a Gnostic. One can only regret that we know so little of so peculiarly interesting a phenomenon. The combination of zeal for the legal observances with bold criticism on the Law as a whole and on its origin reminds us of the Clementines, though it must remain doubtful whether there is any historical connexion.

The Epistle of Barnabas

A word must suffice on two or three books which in one way or another bear on our subject. The *Epistle of Barnabas,* probably written in Hadrian's reign, is a striking example of what the apostolic teaching about the old covenant is *not.* Ignoring the progressive method of God's dealings with mankind, it treats the Jewish practices and beliefs of old time as having always been mere errors, and thus makes the Old Testament into a mere fantastic forestalment of the New Testament. At times we might almost fancy that we hear the teaching of the Sermon on the

Mount or the Epistle of St James, for undeniably the true conception of a law within the Law is there. But all is spoiled by want of sympathy with the true Jewish history and life. If such teaching was common, it could hardly fail to provoke a reaction in favour of Judaistic teaching.

Justin Martyr

More Hellenizing than Judaizing

Hermas and *Justin Martyr*, with whom we may associate the nameless author of the *Didache*, occupy prominent places as examples of Judaizing Christians in that imaginary reconstruction of the history of the Second Century which is required as a basis for those critics who are determined to assign some of the more important books of the New Testament to a late date. In reality nothing could be further from the truth respecting them. The supposition is possible only on the assumption that what was not purely Pauline in the Second Century was either purely Judaistic or else due to an attempt to amalgamate the two tendencies. In reality the great mass of Gentile Christianity, the ancestor of all subsequent Christianities, was none of these things. It accepted and honoured St Paul and his writings, but it understood him very imperfectly, while it was influenced but unconsciously by surrounding ideas and instincts, especially those which soaked in from the Greek world. Not to speak of other such influences, it is worth while to mention the tendency to convert religion into ethics clothed with supernatural sanctions; this being a tendency evidently analogous to Jewish legalism. In a word there was infinitely more Hellenizing than Judaizing. Various writers have seen this of late, but Harnack with especial clearness. Another fact which may mislead is the presence in all three writers of language or ideas which do seem ultimately to be of Jewish origin, but which have no dominating force as regards their views of the relation between the Law and the Gospel, and therefore are in no practical sense Judaistic. The probable source of such accessory tinges of a Jewish or semi-Jewish character is probably to be found in the Jewish Dispersion, which could not fail to furnish many members to the growing Church. Justin Martyr too, as being by birth a Samaritan, must doubtless have come much in contact with the Jewish thought of Palestine, as indeed his *Dialogue* shews.

LECTURE XII

PALESTINIAN EBIONITES

JUSTIN MARTYR'S account[1] of Jewish Christians brings us to a fresh stage in our investigation.

The relations between Jewish and Gentile Christians

Trypho, the Jewish interlocutor, asks him whether a man accepting Jesus as Christ, but desiring to keep the legal ordinances (defined in ch. xlvi. as sabbath-keeping, circumcision, observance of τὰ ἔμμηνα, probably New Moons, and certain ceremonial washings), shall be saved.

In my opinion, says Justin, he will, unless he labours to persuade Gentile converts to keep the same ordinances, declaring that they will not otherwise be saved.

Trypho asking why he says "In my opinion," he replies "There are some who do not venture even to share speech or hospitality with such men: with whom I do not agree." He repeats that Christian keepers of the Law who do not try to force their own

[1] Dialogue with Trypho, cc. 47—48.

ways on Gentile Christians ought, he thinks, to be admitted to fellowship *ὡς ὁμοσπλάγχνοις καὶ ἀδελφοῖς*: but Christian Jews who do exercise such constraint, and refuse fellowship on other terms, "these also in like manner *οὐκ ἀποδέχομαι*"; while those who, remaining Christians, are persuaded by them to adopt the Law, "I suppose shall perhaps also be saved;" but those Christians who for any reason adopt it but deny Jesus to be the Christ, if they do not repent before death, "*οὐδ' ὅλως σωθήσεσθαι ἀποφαίνομαι.*" The same is also his judgment on Jews who before death do not believe on this Messiah, especially if in their synagogues they curse those who have so believed.

Traces of a lower Christology

Here the subject changes, but an important passage soon follows. Trypho calls it a paradoxical statement of Justin's, and incapable of proof, that this Christ pre-existed being God, before the ages, and then was born and became man, without being born *ἄνθρωπος ἐξ ἀνθρώπων.*

Justin recognises the difficulty for Jews; but argues that even if it were so as Trypho said, it might still be true that Jesus was the Christ.

"For there are some," he proceeds, "of our (*leg.* your) race who confess Him to be Christ, yet pronounce Him to be born *ἄνθρωπον ἐξ ἀνθρώπων*; with whom I do not agree: nor would most if they think the same as I do say so, since we have been bidden by the Christ Himself to yield our assent to no merely human teachings, but to truths proclaimed by the blessed prophets and taught by Himself."

The use of *ὁμολογοῦντες*, as many have seen, makes *ὑμετέρου* morally certain (it goes best with *γένους*): so that there is here a clear reference to Christians of Jewish birth who acknowledged our Lord's Messiahship but denied His Divine Nature. It would however be rash to assign them positively, except on external grounds, to any one of the previous classes rather than to another.

No certain evidence of separate sects

There is nothing to shew that those classes were of the nature of sects or in any way separate bodies as multitudes of critics have assumed. This may or may not have been the case. Justin does no more than speak of some Christian keepers of the Law as exclusive, others as not exclusive. The latter would consist of men who simply perpetuated the position of St James: it was probably among such that Hegesippus was brought up. It may be that the intolerant Jewish keepers of the Law formed a distinct community: it may be also that they are identical with those who did not recognise our Lord's Deity: but we have no evidence in Justin that it was so. Unhappily also Justin tells us nothing more about either class: it was not pertinent to his subject to do so. This sentence about the Christology is due as Engelhardt[1] has pointed out to the method of argument which Justin is pursuing, intending in due

[1] Moritz von Engelhardt *Das Christenthum Justins*, p. 275 f.

course to make the argument about Messiahship a stepping stone to a future argument on the higher truth.

The Ebionites

With Irenæus[1] we come to a new name, Ἐβιωναῖοι. They confess, he says, that the world was made by the true God, but in what relates to our Lord they think with Cerinthus and Carpocrates [i.e. doubtless that He was a mere man, without reference to the Gnostic additions]. They use only the Gospel according to Matthew, and reject the Apostle Paul, calling him an apostate from the Law. They endeavour to give curious expositions and prophecies, and they are circumcised and persevere in the customs which are according to the Law and in the Jewish stamp of life, so that they even adore Jerusalem as being the House of God. Of their origin Irenæus says nothing. *Characteristics*

Thence forward the name Ebionæan is of pretty frequent occurrence.

Irenæus's scholar Hippolytus has much the same account, but invents a founder named Ebion. *Hær.* vii. 35

Passing over slight notices in Tertullian and the mere title of a lost book of Clement of Alexandria κανὼν ἐκκλησιαστικὸς ἢ πρὸς τοὺς Ἰουδαΐζοντας, we come to Origen[2] who interprets an obscure phrase of *Origen makes two classes* Eus. *H. E.* vi. 13, 3.

[1] *Adv. Hær.* i. 26, 2.

[2] *Contra Celsum* v. 61.

Celsus about Christian sects as probably meaning "the two kinds of Ebionæans, either like us confessing Jesus to have been born of a Virgin, or [maintaining] that He was not so born, but as other men": in ch. lxv. he says that both kinds rejected St Paul's Epistles. The distinction is made clearer in a comment on Matthew[1] where of Jews believing on Jesus the same two kinds are mentioned, with the addition *οὐ μὴν ἀλλὰ καὶ μετὰ τῆς περὶ αὐτοῦ θεολογίας* in the case of those who accepted the miraculous conception.

H. E. iii. 27. The distinction is carried further still by Eusebius, probably following some lost passage of Origen. He says explicitly that these less heterodox Ebionites did not accept the Lord's pre-existence, as *θεὸς λόγος* and *σοφία*. He repeats that they likewise rejected St Paul and his Epistles, and adds that they used only the Gospel according to the Hebrews (probably a correct statement of what Irenæus loosely calls St Matthew), and that, while like the others they kept the sabbath and other Jewish usages (*ἀγωγήν*), they likewise observed the memory of the Resurrection on the Lord's Day like other Christians.

The two names

In the latter part of the Fourth Century two writers tell us much, Epiphanius and Jerome, not a little from personal acquaintance.

Epiphanius, always a confused writer, here surpasses himself; and his materials have to be picked

[1] *In Mat.* Tom. xvi. 12. Vol. IV. p. 37 f. Lom.

out with the greatest caution. Perhaps he has contributed most to modern confusions by making two separate sects, Ebionæans and Nazaræans.

Both names occur likewise in Jerome's works, and in one famous passage[1] he has been wrongly supposed to distinguish them.

The truth seems to be that Nazaræans was a name used by the Jewish Christians of Syria as a description of themselves in the Fourth Century and probably long before, either taken or inherited from Ac xxiv 5
the designation of the Apostolic age; while Ebionæans, originally an equally genuine popular name (of course representing the Hebrew *Ebionim*, the Poor Men) had become the traditional name for them in Church literature, being either misunderstood to be a proper name, or else (as by Origen) misinterpreted.

That there were at least two grades, so to speak, of Christological doctrine among them is clear from Origen and Eusebius, and perhaps Justin.

But there is no evidence of two distinct communities, much less of the designation of the one as Ebionæans, the other as Nazaræans.

On the other hand it is also clear that one set of them whether divided ecclesiastically from the rest or not, did work out a peculiar system of doctrine and usage. These are the Helxaites, the men of the Clementines, now for the last few years with good reason called Essene Ebionites.

[1] *Ep.* 112, 13.

Probable origin

But to return to the early part of the Second Century. The origin of the main body, whether we call them Ebionæans or Nazaræans, is totally without a record. What seems to me most probable is that they came into existence through the scattering of the old Jerusalem Church by Hadrian's edict, say a third through that century. Besides men of the same mind and position as Hegesippus, men of whom we seem to catch a glimpse also in Justin, it was likely enough that others would be driven into antagonism to the Gentile Church of Asia, and become Judaistic in principle as well as practice. The men like Hegesippus, the maintainers of St James's tradition, when once they had become detached from the Holy City, itself no longer visibly holy, might easily in a generation or two become merged in the great Church without. But this would only the more drive the Judaizers into isolation. It may have been then that they called themselves the Poor Men, probably as claiming to be the true representatives of those who had been blessed in the Sermon on the Mount, but possibly adding to the name other associations. This isolation would diminish the doctrinal influence of other Churches; and the Judaistic position was likely in itself to lead to lower views of our Lord's person, though not necessarily in all cases to the same extent. In this manner the origin and, as far as we know it, the history of Ebionism is, I think, best explained.

Essene Ebionism

The much debated question of the date and origin of the Essene form of Ebionism, that of the Clementines, cannot be properly examined except in connexion with a minute study partly of the extant literature, and still more of the quotations and references in the Fathers. There is, as far as I can see, nothing whatever to connect it with the apostolic age or even the greater part of the second century. The existing works, the Clementine *Homilies* (extant in Greek), and the *Recognitions* (Latin and partly Syriac only), are apparently independent abridgements, for very different purposes, of a voluminous book Περίοδοι Πέτρου, which was current early in the third century. But of earlier (it is said, much earlier) κηρύγματα Πέτρου there is no trace at all; nor does the borrowing of matter from the *Steps of James* by the Clementine writer afford any evidence that these *Steps* were themselves what we may call Clementine (Ebionite they certainly were); so that the date implied in their presumed use by Hegesippus proves little. It is now generally agreed that the book of Helxai, which was brought to the West early in the third century, proceeded from the same body of men. There is a statement that this book professed to be written in the third year of Trajan: but this seems to be due to a misunder-

The 'Clementines' probably not written before 200 A.D.

standing of an extant passage[1], which however obscure and corrupt has nothing to do with the date of the book. There is in fact not a vestige of evidence for either this or the Clementine romance before the third century, and it is probably little if at all older. This literature seems to have proceeded from some great revival among the Ebionites of Eastern Palestine, and its marvellous energy sufficiently attests the force of the movement which gave it birth. The influence of Judaistic Christianity of the ordinary type or types after the apostolic age, as far as our evidence goes, must have been small on the contemporary Church, and almost nothing on posterity. But the strange Clementine literature, whatever may have been its influence, at least found countless readers in East and West. Doubtless it lost some of its most striking features in the various manipulations and adaptations which it underwent: but in one form or another it must from century to century have obtained such a hearing as was given to very few other remains of Antenicene literature.

[1] Hipp. *Omn. Hær. Ref.* ix. 13.

APPENDIX

To page 14

EWALD. *Die drei ersten Evangelien* (2nd Ed.), Vol. I. pp. 263 f.

After commenting on S. Matt. v. 1—16, and noticing how suitably the striking figures of salt and light are there introduced he proceeds:

"This introductory passage fully describes the lofty and unique destiny to which the Twelve are called, and to which they must before all things remain true. It contains also an implicit reference to a Truth, which through the human instruments which propagate it, is to become the salt and light of the earth. It is time therefore to expound this fundamental principle of the New Covenant.

"This fundamental principle, seeing that the attitude in which the New Covenant is to stand to the Old is the all-important question, must be determined essentially by the relation of the New to the Old.

"It might easily be supposed that Christ came to

destroy, i.e. to represent as invalid or of no obligation one of the two parts of the Old Covenant, either the Law or the Prophets, to cancel either the duties prescribed by the Law, or the promises and warnings uttered by the Prophets.

"But the reverse of this is true. He came to fulfil the whole of the Old Covenant (v. 17), to bring about the fulfilment required by its innermost meaning and purpose, with a view to which the germ had been originally implanted in it. So that the New is simply the fulfilment of the Old, and it is in this fulfilment, without any suppression or denial of the Old in the New as though it were something in itself perverted and intolerable, that the New finds its true commencement. Not even the seemingly least significant truth in the O. C. must be sacrificed: nay rather, the precepts of the O. C. are to be far more truly understood and more strictly applied, so that there is nothing more reprehensible than to weaken their obligation by any kind of ingenuity and false interpretation (v. 19) (v. 43 supplies an illustration of this).

"And so it shall be till 'all things are accomplished,' that is till the end of this world, before which event very much that has been prophesied in the O. T. has yet to come to pass (v. 18, to which xxiv. 35 is but partly parallel, while Luke xxi. 32 is merely an epitome of Matt. xxiv. 35).

"It is of course obvious that the imagery in v. 18 (repeated Luke xvi. 17) must be interpreted on the analogy of other great images in the utterances of Jesus.

"Now such a fundamental conception makes two assumptions. First, that Jesus found ready to hand in the O. C. the main outlines of all true religion; he would not therefore himself maintain anything which would contradict them, as indeed we find him constantly stating elsewhere.

"Secondly, that in direct opposition to the traditional method of understanding and applying the O. T. he had formed an entirely different conception of that same perfect religion which, though actually taught by the O. T. had not till then been truly fulfilled and brought into life. As had been already stated (v. 20) an infinitely higher righteousness than that which had been hitherto held to be sufficient must be made to prevail in life.

"In practice however it was evident that if the O. T. either in itself or as it was then legally expounded, contained anything scarcely suited to the spirit of the absolutely true religion, it must be regarded as something that could only receive Divine sanction for its own time and for temporary purposes. This protects Christ from having recourse to the allegorical method which was even then so great a power, and which alas was in later times revived in Christendom after Christ's death."

To page 23

MEUSCHEN. *Nov. Test. ex Talmude...illustratum*, p. 80.

Matth. ix. vers. 15. *Numquid filii thalami lugere possunt quamdiu Sponsus cum illis?*

Propter summum eorum gaudium Talmudici eos liberos esse statuunt ab eis rebus, quae ullo modo gaudium illud impedire possent. Unde in *Suca fol.* 25, 2. Tradiderunt Rabbini: Sponsus, et pronubi, et omnes filii thalami (h. e. hospites nuptiales), liberi sunt ab oratione (*Glossa:* quia ea requirit attentionem), et a locis Oratoriis sibi applicandis (*Glossa:* quia vulgo apud eos reperitur ebrietas et protervia).

To page 71

S. AUG. *c. Faust.* xxxii. 13.

Et in Actibus Apostolorum hoc lege praeceptum ab Apostolis, ut abstinerent gentes tantum a fornicatione et ab immolatis et a sanguine (*Act.* xv. 29), id est, ne quidquam ederent carnis, cujus sanguis non esset effusus. Quod alii non sic intelligunt, sed a sanguine praeceptum esse abstinendum, ne quis homicidio se contaminet. Hoc nunc discutere longum est, et non necessarium: quia et si hoc tunc

Apostoli praeceperunt, ut ab animalium sanguine abstinerent Christiani, ne praefocatis carnibus vescerentur, elegisse mihi videntur pro tempore rem facilem, et nequaquam observantibus onerosam, in qua cum Israelitis etiam Gentes, propter angularem illum lapidem duos in se condentem (*Ephes.* ii. 11—22), aliquid communiter observarent; simul et admonerentur, in ipsa arca Noe, quando Deus hoc jussit, Ecclesiam omnium gentium fuisse figuratam, cujus facti prophetia jam Gentibus ad fidem accedentibus incipiebat impleri. Transacto vero illo tempore, quo illi duo parietes, unus ex circumcisione, alter ex praeputio venientes, quamvis in angulari lapide concordarent, tamen suis quibusdam proprietatibus distinctius eminebant, ac ubi Ecclesia Gentium talis effecta est, ut in ea nullus Israelita carnalis appareat; quis jam hoc Christianus observat, ut turdos vel minutiores aviculas non attingat, nisi quarum sanguis effusus est, aut leporem non edat, si manu a cervice percussus, nullo cruento vulnere occisus est? Et qui forte pauci adhuc tangere ista formidant, a caeteris irridentur: ita omnium animos in hac re tenuit illa sententia veritatis, *Non quod intrat in os vestrum, vos coinquinat, sed quod exit* (*Matt.* xv. 11); nullam cibi naturam, quam societas admittit humana, sed quae iniquitas committit peccata, condemnans.

To page 72

EWALD. *Antiquities of Israel*, pp. 37 f.
(*Alterth.* III. 51 f.)

"This symbol [for bringing clearly before the senses the awfulness of the whole proceeding in the case of an animal sacrifice] was furnished by the *blood*, which to a great portion of remote Antiquity appeared to have about it something so utterly mysterious, so divinely sacred, that a belief became deeply rooted that true sacrifice could be carried out perfectly only by means of its intervention. A strong feeling of this had already completely transformed the whole department of sacrifice among the people of Israel, in times which we must consider as relatively very early; and the Book of Origins still depicts for us vividly enough the feeling in this matter which for many centuries penetrated the ancient nation.

"Indeed the warm blood of men, and of quadrupeds and birds, seemed to contain the very soul or life of the living earthly creature—to be almost identical with its soul. The Book of Origins hardly knows how to put this sufficiently strongly in the passages devoted to it [Levit. xvii. 11, Gen. ix. 5]. Now when the life and the soul were held to be something sacred, and the more tender feelings of certain nations took this view very early, it would follow that the blood too must be considered a sacred thing, and be regarded quite differently from the rest of the body. The sight of that which was held to be the soul itself, carried the mind immediately to thoughts of God, placed directly before it something full of mystery, and filled it with that immeasurably profound awe which overpowers man whenever he sees any rent in the veil between him and the Divine. In accordance with such feelings, blood could be scarcely touched, still less eaten by pious men; and ancient Jahveism impressed its immunity in every way as deeply as possible. Even the inviolability of human life received support from the sanctity of the blood. To taste the minutest portion of animal blood was something horrible; even the blood of such animals as were allowed for eating, but not for sacrifice, was to be poured 'like water' upon the ground, and covered over with earth."

To page 73

ORIG. *c. Cels.* viii. 30.

Τὸ μὲν γὰρ εἰδωλόθυτον θύεται δαιμονίοις· καὶ οὐ χρὴ τὸν τοῦ θεοῦ ἄνθρωπον κοινωνὸν τραπέζης δαιμονίων γίνεσθαι· τὰ δὲ πνικτὰ τοῦ αἵματος μὴ ἐκκριθέντος, ὅπερ φασὶν εἶναι τροφὴν δαιμόνων, τρεφομένων ταῖς ἀπ' αὐτοῦ ἀναθυμιάσεσιν, ἀπαγορεύει ὁ λόγος, ἵνα μὴ τραφῶμεν τροφῇ δαιμόνων· τάχα τινῶν τοιούτων πνευμάτων συντραφησομένων ἡμῖν, ἐὰν μεταλαμβάνωμεν *τῶν πνικτῶν. Ἐκ δὲ τῶν εἰρημένων περὶ τῶν πνικτῶν σαφὲς εἶναι δύναται τὸ περὶ τῆς ἀποχῆς τοῦ αἵματος.*

To page 140

WEBER. *Syst. d. alt. Syn. Pal. Theol.* 101 f.

The doctrine contained in the Thora cannot be elicited (*herausgestellt*) until in the conflict with contradictions it unfolds itself and declares that the Wise [i.e. the Scribes] lay down mutually contradictory decisions. The Jewish theology solves this difficulty in the way of the Divine authoritative character of the oral tradition by referring the contradictions to the multiplicity of sense in the written Thora.

We read *Erubin* 13[b] 'Three years did the school of Shammai and Hillel strive together, and when both sides declared that their interpretation must rank as Halacha, there came a Revelation from heaven and said: Both are God's word; but the doctrine of the school of Hillel ranks as Halacha.'

The school of Hillel were according to *Jebamoth* 14[a] the more numerous and the more popular school, and therefore their doctrinal system prevailed. An old oft-repeated aphorism occurs *Tosefta Sota* c. 7: "All words are given from one shepherd, One God has supplied them all, One Shepherd has given them, the Lord of all that is made, blessed be He, has spoken them. Do thou also make thine heart many chambers and store therein the words of Hillel and of Shammai, the words of those who declare clean and of those who declare unclean."

The Midrash often says the same, e.g. *Bammidbar rabba* c. 14, cf. *Chagiga* 3[b]: "They all (these contradictory doctrines of the Wise) have been given by One God, and one Pastor (Moses) uttered them from the mouth of the Lord."

Tanchuma, Behaalothecha 15 explains the facts more precisely: 'All the utterances of the Wise are derived from the one Moses and the One God; the one hath this decree, the other that; i.e., one Wise man can appeal for his interpretation to this passage of Scripture, the other to that. These differences of doctrine do not on that account produce any disunion. The schools of Hillel and of Shammai, though they took very different views on questions connected with marriage, did not refuse to intermarry, and though they took very different lines on questions of clean and unclean they suffered no inconvenience on that account in the intercourse of life.' *Jebamoth* 14[b].

The *Bath Kol* is introduced with a view to the final solution of particular disputes—but as an exception to the rule, and only in specially important questions. In other cases the decision whether an opinion was or was not in accordance with prevailing views was ruled by the principle 'there is no *Halacha* but according to the decision of the majority.'

In the days of Messiah Elijah will come to finally

adjust the controversies that remain undetermined. And so a discussion which leads to no decision is closed by the word תיקו which means that further discussion must be postponed. The derivation of this word is doubtful...but the formula is of importance as showing that in the developed teaching of the oral Thora there remained details, which were to be left undecided for the present. The oral Thora remains open, while the written Thora is complete.

The passage from 'the Chagiga' referred to above runs as follows in Mr Streane's translation p. 9. It occurs in a discussion of Eccles. xii. 11.

"Masters of Assemblies." These are the disciples of wise men, who sit by companies and study in the Law, some declaring unclean and others declaring clean, some binding and others loosing, some disqualifying and others pronouncing ceremonially pure.

"Perhaps a man may say, How under these circumstances [seeing that experts thus differ] am I to learn the Law?

"The teaching says, All of them 'are given from one shepherd.' One God gave them, one pastor uttered them from the mouth of the Lord of all that is made, blessed be He, for it is written, 'and God spake all these words.' Also do thou make thine ear as the upper millstone, and procure for thyself an understanding heart to hear the words of those who declare unclean and the words of those who declare clean, the words of those who bind and the words of those who loose, the words of those who disqualify and the words of those who pronounce ceremonially pure."

To page 162

HERMAE *Pastor. Sim.* ix. 17.

'Now then, Sir, explain to me concerning the mountains. Wherefore are their forms diverse the one from the other, and various?' 'Listen,' saith he. 'These twelve mountains are [twelve] tribes that inhabit the whole world. To these (tribes) then the Son of God was preached by the Apostles.' 'But explain to me, Sir, why these are various—these mountains—and each has a different appearance.' 'Listen,' saith he. 'These twelve tribes which inhabit the whole world are twelve nations; and they are various in understanding and in mind. As various, then, as thou sawest these mountains to be, such also are the varieties in the mind of these nations, and such their understanding. And I will show unto thee the conduct of each.' 'First, Sir,' say I, 'show me this, why the mountains being so various, yet, when their stones were set into the building, became bright and of one colour, just like the stones that had come up from the deep.' 'Because,' saith he, 'all the nations that dwell under heaven, when they heard and believed, were called by the one name of [the

Son of] God. So having received the seal, they had one understanding and one mind, and one faith became theirs and [one] love, and they bore the spirits of the virgins along with the Name; therefore the building of the tower became of one colour, even bright as the sun. But after they entered in together, and became one body, some of them defiled themselves, and were cast out from the society of the righteous, and became again such as they were before, or rather even worse.'

(From LIGHTFOOT and HARMER. *Apostolic Fathers.*)

INDEX OF PASSAGES QUOTED

OLD TESTAMENT

NEW TESTAMENT

PATRISTIC AND HELLENISTIC